Love & Best
Wishes, 17/9/93
Bob xx

PHILIP'S

FAMILY
WORLD
ATLAS

First published in Great Britain in 1993
by George Philip Limited,
an imprint of Reed Consumer Books Limited,
Michelin House, 81 Fulham Road, London SW3 6RB
and Auckland, Melbourne, Singapore and Toronto

Copyright © 1993 Reed International Books Limited

ISBN 0 540 05728 2

A CIP catalogue record for this book is available from
the British Library

Printed in Hong Kong

CONTENTS

iv   **World Statistics: Countries**

I   **Key to Map Symbols**

2–3   **The World: Political** 1:80M

4   **The Arctic and Antarctica** 1:50M

5   **Europe: Political** 1:20M

6–7   **Scandinavia and the Baltic Lands** 1:5M

8–9   **England and Wales** 1:2M

10   **Scotland** 1:2M

11   **Ireland** 1:2M

12   **France** 1:5M

13   **Spain and Portugal** 1:5M

14–15   **Italy and the Balkans** 1:5M

16–17   **Central Europe** 1:5M

18–19   **Eastern Europe, Russia and Central Asia** 1:20M

20   **Asia: Political** 1:50M

21   **Japan** 1:10M
         Southern Japan 1:5M

22   **China** 1:20M

23   **South-east Asia** 1:20M

24   **Southern Asia** 1:20M

25   **South-west Asia** 1:20M

26–27   **Northern Africa** 1:15M

28–29   **Central and Southern Africa** 1:15M

30   **Africa: Political** 1:40M

31   **New Zealand** 1:6M
         Fiji, Tonga and Samoan Islands 1:12M

32–33   **Australia** 1:12M

34–35   **Canada** 1:15M
         Alaska 1:30M

36–37   **United States** 1:12M
         Hawaii 1:10M

38–39   **Mexico, Central America and the West Indies** 1:15M
         Leeward Islands, Windward Islands, Trinidad and Tobago, and Jamaica 1:5M

40–41   **South America – North** 1:16M

42   **South America – South** 1:16M

43–48   **Index**

WORLD STATISTICS: COUNTRIES

This alphabetical list includes all the countries and territories of the world. If a territory is not completely independent, then the country it is associated with is named. The area figures give the total area of land, inland water and ice. Units for areas and populations are thousands. The figures are the latest available, usually 1991.

Country/Territory	Area km² Thousands	Population Thousands	Capital
Afghanistan	652	16,433	Kabul
Albania	28.8	3,250	Tirana
Algeria	2,382	24,960	Algiers
American Samoa (US)	0.20	39	Pago Pago
Andorra	0.45	52	Andorre-la-Vella
Angola	1,247	10,020	Luanda
Anguilla (UK)	0.40	8	The Valley
Antigua & Barbuda	0.44	77	St John's
Argentina	2,767	32,322	Buenos Aires
Armenia	29.8	3,416	Yerevan
Aruba (Neths.)	0.19	60	Oranjestad
Australia	7,687	17,086	Canberra
Austria	83.9	7,712	Vienna
Azerbaijan	86.6	7,451	Baku
Azores (Port)	2.2	260	Ponta Delgada
Bahamas	13.9	253	Nassau
Bahrain	0.68	503	Manama
Bangladesh	144	115,594	Dacca
Barbados	0.43	255	Bridgetown
Belau (US)	0.46	15	Koror
Belgium	30.5	9,845	Brussels
Belize	23	188	Belmopan
Belorussia	207.6	10,374	Minsk
Benin	113	4,736	Porto-Novo
Bermuda (UK)	0.05	61	Hamilton
Bhutan	47	1,517	Thimphu
Bolivia	1,099	7,400	La Paz/Sucre
Bosnia-Herzegovina	51.2	4,364	Sarajevo
Botswana	582	1,291	Gaborone
Brazil	8,512	153,322	Brasilia
Brunei	5.8	266	Bandar Seri Begawan
Bulgaria	111	9,011	Sofia
Burkina Faso	274	9,001	Ouagadougou
Burma (Myanmar)	677	41,675	Rangoon
Burundi	27.8	5,438	Bujumbura
Cambodia	181	8,246	Phnom Penh
Cameroon	475	11,834	Yaoundé
Canada	9,976	26,522	Ottawa
Canary Is. (Spain)	7.3	1,700	Las Palmas/Santa Cruz
Cape Verde Is.	4	370	Praia
Cayman Is. (UK)	0.26	27	Georgetown
Central African Rep.	623	3,039	Bangui
Chad	1,284	5,679	Ndjamena
Chile	757	13,386	Santiago
China	9,597	1,139,060	Beijing (Peking)
Colombia	1,139	32,987	Bogotá
Comoros	2.2	551	Moroni
Congo	342	2,271	Brazzaville
Cook Is. (NZ)	0.24	18	Avarua
Costa Rica	51.1	2,994	San José
Croatia	56.5	4,784	Zagreb
Cuba	111	10,609	Havana
Cyprus	9.3	702	Nicosia
Czech Republic	78.9	10,299	Prague
Denmark	43.1	5,140	Copenhagen
Djibouti	23.2	409	Djibouti
Dominica	0.75	83	Roseau
Dominican Republic	48.7	7,170	Santo Domingo
Ecuador	284	10,782	Quito
Egypt	1,001	53,153	Cairo
El Salvador	21	5,252	San Salvador
Equatorial Guinea	28.1	348	Malabo
Estonia	44.7	1,600	Tallinn
Ethiopia	1,222	50,974	Addis Ababa
Falkland Is. (UK)	12.2	2	Stanley
Faroe Is. (Den.)	1.4	47	Tórshavn
Fiji	18.3	765	Suva
Finland	338	4,986	Helsinki
France	552	56,440	Paris
French Guiana (Fr.)	90	99	Cayenne
French Polynesia (Fr.)	4	206	Papeete
Gabon	268	1,172	Libreville
Gambia, The	11.3	861	Banjul
Georgia	69.7	5,571	Tbilisi.
Germany	357	79,479	Berlin
Ghana	239	15,028	Accra
Gibraltar (UK)	0.007	31	-
Greece	132	10,269	Athens
Greenland (Den.)	2,176	60	Godthåb
Grenada	0.34	85	St George's
Guadeloupe (Fr.)	1.7	344	Basse-Terre
Guam (US)	0.55	119	Agana
Guatemala	109	9,197	Guatemala City
Guinea	246	5,756	Conakry
Guinea-Bissau	36.1	965	Bissau
Guyana	215	796	Georgetown
Haiti	27.8	6,486	Port-au-Prince
Honduras	112	5,105	Tegucigalpa
Hong Kong (UK)	1.1	5,801	-
Hungary	93	10,344	Budapest
Iceland	103	255	Reykjavik
India	3,288	843,931	Delhi
Indonesia	1,905	179,300	Jakarta
Iran	1,648	58,031	Tehran
Iraq	438	18,920	Baghdad
Ireland	70.3	3,523	Dublin
Israel	27	4,659	Jerusalem
Italy	301	57,663	Rome
Ivory Coast	322	11,998	Abidjan
Jamaica	11	2,420	Kingston
Japan	378	123,537	Tokyo
Jordan	89.2	4,009	Amman
Kazakhstan	2,717	17,104	Alma Ata
Kenya	580	24,032	Nairobi
Kirghizia	198.5	4,568	Bishkek
Kiribati	0.72	66	Tarawa
Korea, North	121	21,773	Pyongyang
Korea, South	99	43,302	Seoul
Kuwait	17.8	2,143	Kuwait City
Laos	237	4,139	Vientiane
Latvia	63.1	2,700	Riga
Lebanon	10.4	2,701	Beirut
Lesotho	30.4	1,774	Maseru
Liberia	111	2,607	Monrovia
Libya	1,760	4,545	Tripoli
Liechtenstein	0.16	29	Vaduz
Lithuania	65.2	3,751	Vilnius
Luxembourg	2.6	384	Luxembourg
Macau (Port.)	0.02	479	-
Macedonia	25.3	2,174	Skopje
Madagascar	587	11,197	Antananarivo
Madeira (Port.)	0.81	280	Funchal
Malawi	118	8,556	Lilongwe
Malaysia	330	17,861	Kuala Lumpur
Maldives	0.30	215	Malé
Mali	1,240	8,156	Bamako
Malta	0.32	354	Valletta
Mariana Is. (US)	0.48	22	Saipan
Marshall Is. (US)	0.18	42	Majuro
Martinique (Fr.)	1.1	341	Fort-de-France
Mauritania	1,025	2,050	Nouakchott
Mauritius	1.9	1,075	Port Louis
Mayotte (Fr.)	0.37	84	Mamoundzou
Mexico	1,958	86,154	Mexico City
Micronesia, Fed. St. (US)	0.70	103	Kolonia
Moldavia	33.7	4,458	Kishinev
Monaco	0.002	29	-
Mongolia	1,567	2,190	Ulan Bator
Montserrat (UK)	0.10	13	Plymouth
Morocco	447	25,061	Rabat
Mozambique	802	15,656	Maputo
Namibia	824	1,781	Windhoek
Nauru	0.02	10	Domaneab
Nepal	141	18,916	Katmandu
Netherlands	41.9	15,019	Amsterdam
Neths. Antilles (Neths.)	0.99	189	Willemstad
New Caledonia (Fr.)	19	168	Nouméa
New Zealand	269	3,429	Wellington
Nicaragua	130	3,871	Managua
Niger	1,267	7,732	Niamey
Nigeria	924	108,542	Lagos/Abuja
Norway	324	4,242	Oslo
Oman	212	1,502	Muscat
Pakistan	796	112,050	Islamabad
Panama	77.1	2,418	Panama City
Papua New Guinea	463	3,699	Port Moresby
Paraguay	407	4,277	Asunción
Peru	1,285	22,332	Lima
Philippines	300	61,480	Manila
Poland	313	38,180	Warsaw
Portugal	92.4	10,525	Lisbon
Puerto Rico (US)	8.9	3,599	San Juan
Qatar	11	368	Doha
Réunion (Fr.)	2.5	599	St-Denis
Romania	238	23,200	Bucharest
Russia	17,075	149,527	Moscow
Rwanda	26.3	7,181	Kigali
St Christopher/Nevis	0.36	44	Basseterre
St Lucia	0.62	151	Castries
St Pierre & Miquelon (Fr.)	0.24	6	St Pierre
St Vincent/Grenadines	0.39	116	Kingstown
San Marino	0.06	24	San Marino
São Tomé & Príncipe	0.96	121	São Tomé
Saudi Arabia	2,150	14,870	Riyadh
Senegal	197	7,327	Dakar
Seychelles	0.46	67	Victoria
Sierra Leone	71.7	4,151	Freetown
Singapore	0.62	3,003	Singapore
Slovak Republic	49	5,269	Bratislava
Slovenia	20.3	1,963	Ljubljana
Solomon Is.	28.9	321	Honiara
Somalia	638	7,497	Mogadishu
South Africa	1,221	35,282	Pretoria
Spain	505	38,959	Madrid
Sri Lanka	65.6	16,993	Colombo
Sudan	2,506	25,204	Khartoum
Surinam	163	422	Paramaribo
Swaziland	17.4	768	Mbabane
Sweden	450	8,618	Stockholm
Switzerland	41.3	6,712	Bern
Syria	185	12,116	Damascus
Taiwan	36	20,300	Taipei
Tajikistan	143.1	5,680	Dushanbe
Tanzania	945	25,635	Dar es Salaam
Thailand	513	57,196	Bangkok
Togo	56.8	3,531	Lomé
Tonga	0.75	95	Nuku'alofa
Trinidad & Tobago	5.1	1,227	Port of Spain
Tunisia	164	8,180	Tunis
Turkey	779	57,326	Ankara
Turkmenistan	488.1	3,838	Ashkhabad
Turks & Caicos Is. (UK)	0.43	10	Grand Turk
Tuvalu	0.03	10	Funafuti
Uganda	236	18,795	Kampala
Ukraine	603.7	51,940	Kiev
United Arab Emirates	83.6	1,589	Abu Dhabi
United Kingdom	243.3	54,889	London
United States	9,373	249,928	Washington
Uruguay	177	3,094	Montevideo
Uzbekistan	447.4	21,627	Tashkent
Vanuatu	12.2	147	Port Vila
Venezuela	912	19,735	Caracas
Vietnam	332	66,200	Hanoi
Virgin Is. (UK)	0.15	13	Road Town
Virgin Is. (US)	0.34	117	Charlotte Amalie
Wallis & Futuna Is. (Fr.)	0.20	18	Mata-Utu
Western Sahara (Mor.)	266	179	El Aiun
Western Samoa	2.8	164	Apia
Yemen	528	11,282	Sana
Yugoslavia	102.3	10,642	Belgrade
Zaïre	2,345	35,562	Kinshasa
Zambia	753	8,073	Lusaka
Zimbabwe	391	9,369	Harare

GENERAL REFERENCE

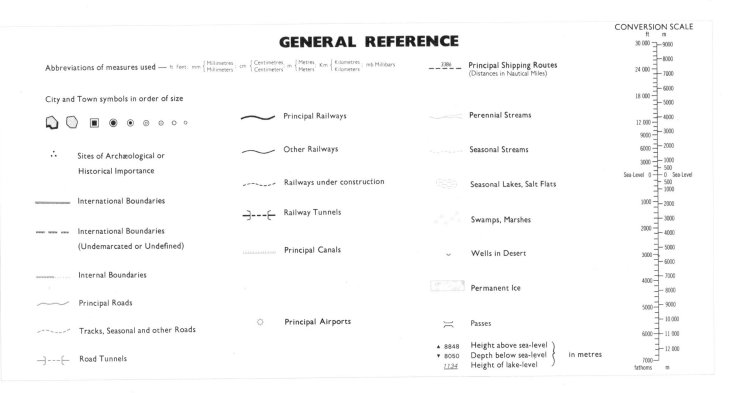

Abbreviations of measures used — ft Feet: mm {Millimetres / Millimeters} : cm {Centimetres / Centimeters} : m {Metres / Meters} Km {Kilometres / Kilometers} mb Millibars

City and Town symbols in order of size

∴ Sites of Archæological or Historical Importance

International Boundaries

International Boundaries (Undemarcated or Undefined)

Internal Boundaries

Principal Roads

Tracks, Seasonal and other Roads

Road Tunnels

Principal Railways

Other Railways

Railways under construction

Railway Tunnels

Principal Canals

Principal Airports

3386 Principal Shipping Routes (Distances in Nautical Miles)

Perennial Streams

Seasonal Streams

Seasonal Lakes, Salt Flats

Swamps, Marshes

Wells in Desert

Permanent Ice

Passes

▲ 8848 Height above sea-level
▼ 8050 Depth below sea-level } in metres
_1134_ Height of lake-level

CONVERSION SCALE
ft / m
30 000 — 9000
— 8000
24 000 — 7000
— 6000
18 000 — 5000
— 4000
12 000 — 3000
9000 — 2000
6000 — 1000
3000 — 500
Sea-Level 0 — 0 Sea-Level
500
1000 — 1000
2000
2000 — 3000
4000
3000 — 5000
6000
4000 — 7000
8000
5000 — 9000
10 000
6000 — 11 000
12 000
7000
fathoms m

THE WORLD
Physical
1:150 000 000

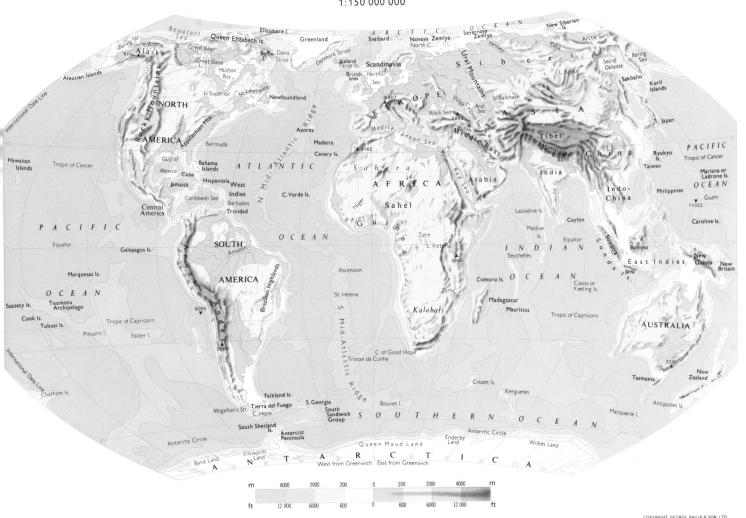

Projection: *Hammer Equal Area*

m 4000 2000 200 0 200 2000 4000 m
ft 12 000 6000 600 0 600 6000 12 000 ft

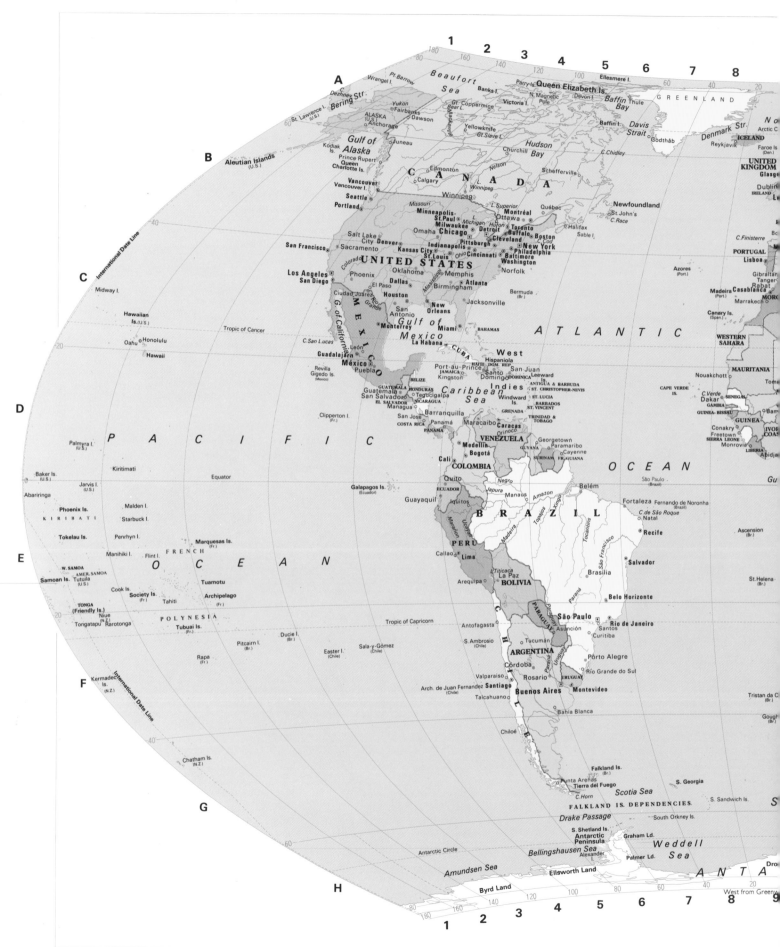

Projection: *Hammer Equal Area*

ARCTIC OCEAN

Scale markings (top): 0 11 12 13 14 15 16 17 18
160 180 80
40 60 80 100 120 140

albard
(Norway)
n Narvik
Zemlya Frantsa Iosifa
Novaya Zemlya
New Siberian Is.
East Siberian
Sea
Laptev Sea
Severnaya
Zemlya
A
Barents Sea
Nord Kapp
Kara
Sea
Ust Port
Tiksi
Arctic Circle
Anadyr

Murmansk
Arkhangelsk
Salekhard
Yenisey
Verkhoyansk
Nizhne-Kolymsk

SWEDEN
FINLAND
Helsinki
St. Peterburg
Ob
Lena
Bering
Sea
Oslo
Stockholm
EST
Yaroslavl
Perm
Yekaterinburg
Tomsk
Krasnoyarsk
Vilyuysk
Yakutsk
Okhotsk
Kamchatka
Petropavlovsk-
Kamchatskiy
B
Narvik
NORWAY
DENMARK
Kazan
Uta
Chelyabinsk
Omsk
R U S S I A
L.Baykal
Irtysh
Sakhalin
C.Lopatka

enhavn
Hamburg
Berlin
POLAND Warszawa
Minsk
Samara
Novosibirsk
Novokuznetsk
Barnaul
Irkutsk
Ulan
Ude
Komsomolsk
Khabarovsk
Sea of
Okhotsk
Kuril Is.

Praha
GERM
Kiyev
Voronezh
Saratov
Orenburg
KAZAKHSTAN
Karaganda
Ulaanbaatar
Amur
Vladivostok
Sapporo
Hakodate

Wien
Budapest
Lvov
UKRAINE
Volga
Volgograd
L.Balkhash
MONGOLIA
Harbin
Changchun
Shenyang
N.KOREA
Pyŏngyang
Sea of
Japan
JAPAN
Tōkyō
C

Milano
ROMANIA
Rostov
Astrakhan
Aral
Sea
Alma Ata
Beijing
Tianjin
Dalian
Sŏul
S.KOREA
Kyoto
Yokohama
Nagoya

Beograd
Bucuresti
Black
Sea
Grozny
Tbilisi
UZBEKISTAN
KIRGHIZIA
Taiyuan
Xi'an
Jinan
Qingdao
Pusan
Kōbe
Ōsaka

Roma
BULGARIA
Sofiya
Istanbul
Yerevan
Baku
Samarkand
Tashkent
C H I N A
Huang
Kitakyūshū

Barcelona
GREECE
Athinai
Ankara
TURKEY
ARM
GEO.
TURKMENISTAN
Dushanbe
TAJ.
Lanzhou
Wuhan
Nanjing
Shanghai
East China
Sea

cia
Sardinia
Izmir
Halab
SYRIA
Baghdad
Tehrān
Mashhad
Chengdu
Chongqing
Changsha
Fuzhou
PACIFIC

Tunis
Sicily
MALTA
Crete
CYPRUS
Dimashq
IRAQ
IRAN
AFGHANISTAN
Kabul
XIZANG
(TIBET)
Lhasa
Kunming
Taibei
TAIWAN

Tarābulus
Tel Aviv-Yafo
Amman
Esfahan
Rawalpindi
Lahore
Delhi
NEPAL
Kathmandu
Guangzhou
Hong Kong
Tropic of Cancer

LIBYA
EGYPT
El Iskandariya
El Qahira
ISR
JORDAN
Bur Said
KUWAIT
Ābādān
Shiraz
PAKISTAN
Agra
Kanpur
Lucknow
BANGLA-
DESH
Dhaka
BURMA
Fuzhou
Hainan
Hanoi
OCEAN

O C E A N
The Gulf
BAHRAIN
QATAR
U.A.E.
Karachi
INDIA
Ganga
Calcutta
(MYANMAR)
Mandalay
Wake I.
(U.S.)

Salah
Ar Riyād
SAUDI
ARABIA
Makkah
Aswān
Red
Sea
OMAN
Ahmadabad
Arabian
Bombay
Nagpur
Pune
Bay of
Bengal
Rangoon
NORTHERN
MARIANAS

NIGER
CHAD
Omdurmān
El Khartūm
YEMEN
Aden
Socotra
(Yemen)
Sea
Hyderabad
THAILAND
Bangkok
Manila
Guam
(U.S.)
D

mey
Kano
Ndjamena
SUDAN
White Nile
Asmera
DJIBOUTI
Gulf of Aden
Bangalore
Madras
Andaman Is.
(India)
CAMBODIA
Phnom
Penh
PHILIPPINES
Cebu
MARSHALL IS.

NIGERIA
Ibadan
Lagos
CENTRAL
AFRICAN
REPUBLIC
Addis Abeba
ETHIOPIA
Lakshadweep Is.
Nicobar Is.
(India)
Phanh Bho
Ho Chi Minh
Yap
FEDERATED STATES

Douala
Yaoundé
Bangui
SOMALI REP.
Colombo
SRI LANKA
(CEYLON)
BELAU
Caroline Is.
Truk
Ponape
OF MICRONESIA

RIAL GUINEA
Libreville
TOME
PRINCIPE
GABON
ZAIRE
(CONGO)
Kisangani
UGANDA
Kampala
KENYA
Muqdisho
MALDIVES
Dondra Hd.
MALAYSIA
BRUNEI
Kuala Lumpur
SABAH
NAURU
Gilbert Is.

CABINDA
Zaire
(Congo)
Kasai
Kinshasa
Kananga
Victoria
BUR.
Nairobi
Equator
Medan
PEN. MALAYSIA
SINGAPORE
Kuching
KIRIBATI

Brazzaville
ANGOLA
L.
Tanganyika
TANZANIA
Mombasa
Zanzibar
Dar es Salaam
SEYCHELLES
Amirante
Is.
I N D I A N
Palembang
Sumatera
Banjarmasin
Sulawesi
Borneo
Maluku
Irian
Jaya
New Ireland
Rabaul

Luanda
Lubumbashi
COMORO
IS.
Aldabra
Chagos Arch.
(Br.)
Surabaya
INDONESIA
PAPUA
NEW
GUINEA
New
Britain
SOLOMON
IS.

Benguela
ZAMBIA
Lusaka
MALAWI
Malawi
Diego Garcia
(Br.)
O C E A N
Jakarta
Bandung
Jawa
Ujung Pandang
Timor
Port
Moresby
Louisade
Arch.
TUVALU

NAMIBIA
ZIMBABWE
Harare
MOZAMBIQUE
Antananarivo
MADAGASCAR
Rodriguez
Cocos
(Keeling Is.)
(Australia)
Christmas I.
(Australia)
Islands
Arafura Sea
Timor
Sea
C.York
Darwin
Santa Cruz Is.
E

Bulawayo
BOTSWANA
Mozambique Chan.
MAURITIUS
Réunion
(Fr.)
Tropic of Capricorn
North West C.
NORTHERN
TERRITORY
WESTERN
Townsville
Cairns
VANUATU
Vanua Levu
Viti Levu
Suva
FIJI

Windhoek
SOUTH
Gaborone
Pretoria
Johannesburg
SWAZ.
Maputo
QUEENSLAND
Alice Springs
AUSTRALIA
Rockhampton
New
Caledonia
(Fr.)
20

Cape Town
C.of Good Hope
Port Elizabeth
SOUTH
AFRICA
LES.
Durban
Amsterdam
(Fr.)
St.Paul
(Fr.)
C.Leeuwin
Perth
Fremantle
Kalgoorlie-
Boulder
SOUTH
AUSTRALIA
Great
Australian
Bight
Adelaide
NEW SOUTH
WALES
Newcastle
Sydney
Lord Howe
I.
(Australia)
Norfolk I.
(Australia)
F

Pr.Edward Is.
(South Africa)
Crozet Is.
(Fr.)
Kerguelen
(Fr.)
McDonald I.
(Australia)
Heard I.
(Australia)
VICTORIA
Melbourne
Canberra
Darling
Tasman
Sea
Auckland
North I.
NEW
ZEALAND
C.Farewell
Christchurch

ouvet I.
(Norway)
TASMANIA
Hobart
South I.
Dunedin
Stewart I.
Bounty Is.
(N.Z.)
Antipodes Is.
(N.Z.)

OUTHERN
OCEAN
Macquarie I.
(Australia)
Campbell I.
(N.Z.)
Auckland I.
(N.Z.)
G

CTICA
ast from Greenwich
Enderby
Land
Wilkes Land
S. Magnetic Pole
Balleny Is.
Ross Sea
H

Scale markings (bottom): 0 11 12 13 14 15 16 17 18
20 40 60 80 100 120 140 160 180 80

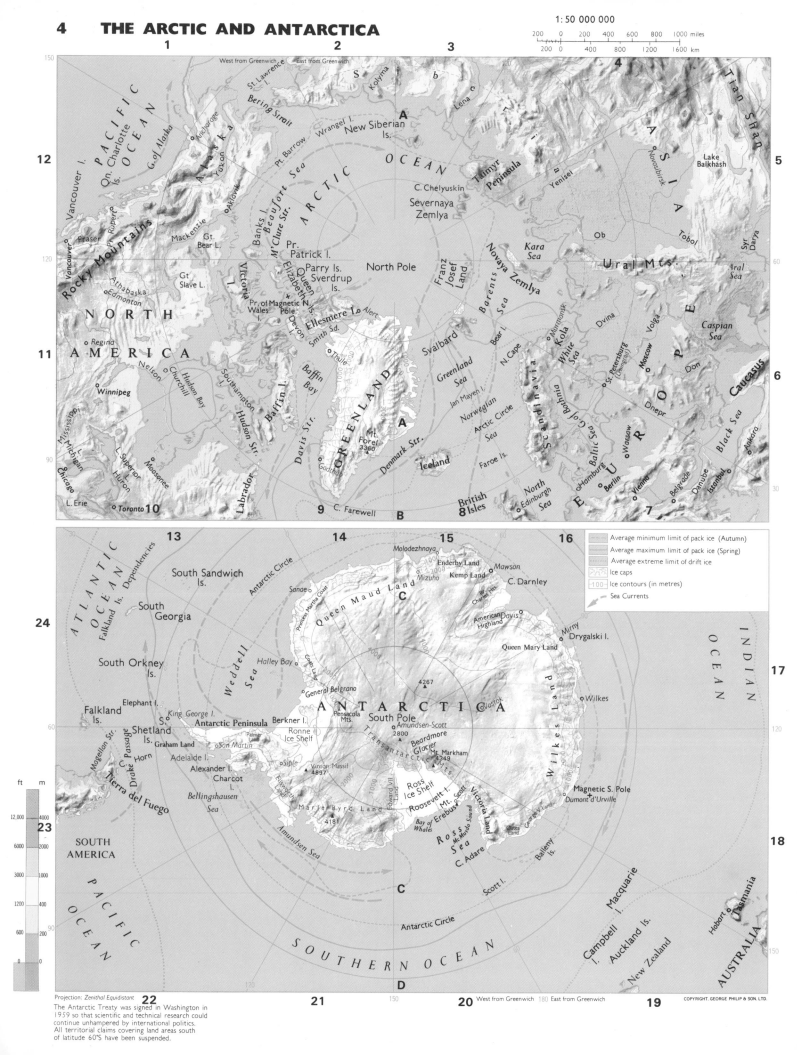

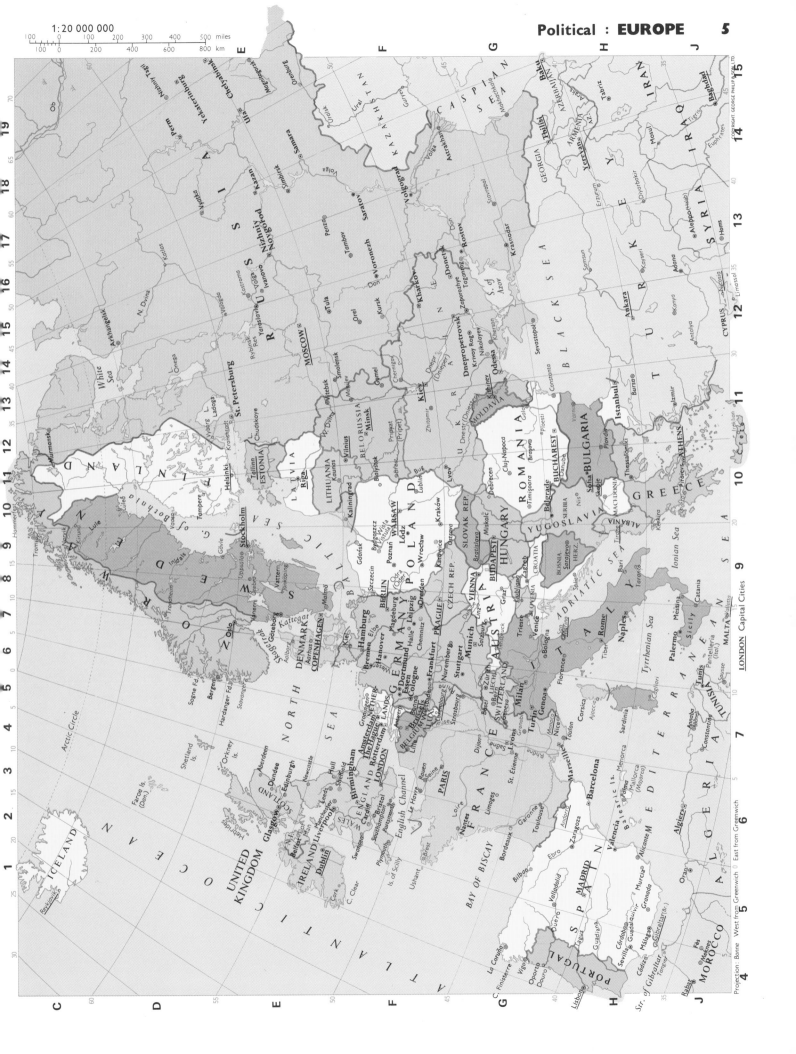

1:20 000 000

Projection: Bonne

LONDON Capital Cities

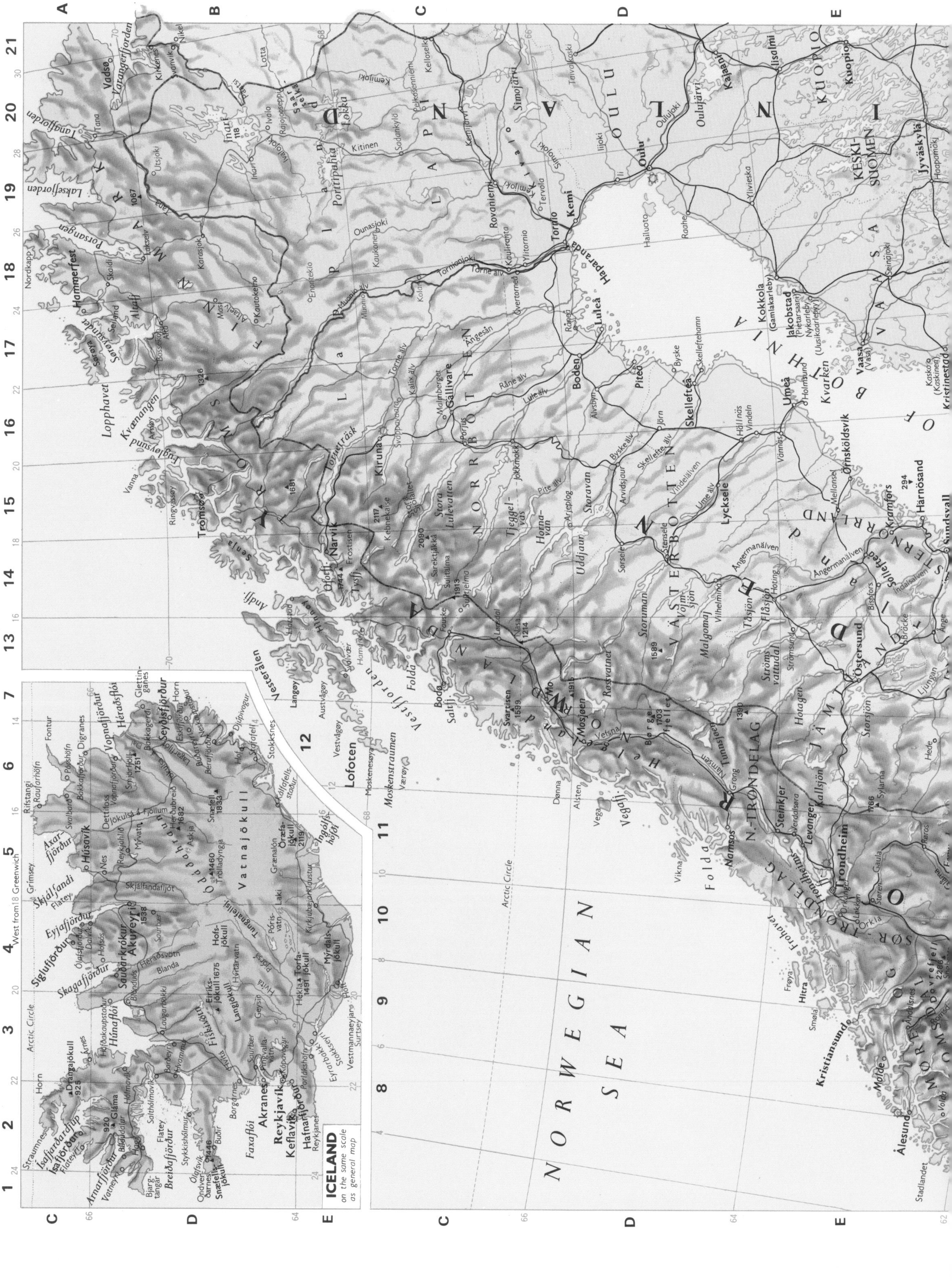

ICELAND
on the same scale
as general map

West from 18 Greenwich

Arctic Circle

NORWEGIAN SEA

LAPPLAND

FINLAND

OULU

KESKI-SUOMEN

GULF OF BOTHNIA

NORRBOTTEN

VÄSTERBOTTEN

VÄSTERNORRLAND

JÄMTLAND

N-TRÖNDELAG

SØR-TRÖNDELAG

Reykjavik
Keflavik
Akranes
Hafnarfjördur
Husavik
Akureyri
Siglufjördur
Vatnajökull
Vestmannaeyjar
Surtsey

Vadsø
Hammerfest
Tromsø
Narvik
Lofoten
Vesterålen
Bodø
Mo
Mosjøen
Namsos
Steinkjer
Levanger
Trondheim
Kristiansund
Molde
Ålesund

Kiruna
Gällivare
Boden
Luleå
Piteå
Skellefteå
Umeå
Örnsköldsvik
Härnösand
Östersund

Oulu
Kemi
Rovaniemi
Haparanda
Kokkola (Gamlakarleby)
Jakobstad (Pietarsaari)
Vaasa (Vasa)
Jyväskylä
Kuopio
Iisalmi
Kajaani

Arctic Circle

NORTH SEA

IRISH SEA

SCOTLAND

Southern Uplands

Cheviot Hills

NORTHUMBERLAND

CUMBRIA

Pennines

DURHAM

TYNE & WEAR

CLEVELAND

N. York Moors

NORTH YORKSHIRE

WEST YORKSHIRE

SOUTH YORKSHIRE

HUMBERSIDE

Holderness

LINCOLN

Lincoln Wolds

NOTTS

DERBY

LANCASHIRE

MERSEYSIDE

CHESHIRE

STAFFORD

CLWYD

GWYNEDD

Anglesey

Snowdon 1085

Cumbrian Mts.

Sca Fell 978

Skiddaw 931

Helvellyn 950

Cross Fell 893

ISLE OF MAN

Snaefell 620

The Wash

The Broads

Cromer

North Walsham

Sandringham

Fakenham

Kings Lynn

Hunstanton

Wells

Skegness

Mablethorpe

Alford

Louth

Horncastle

Market Rasen

Gainsborough

Spalding

Bourne

Grantham

Sleaford

Newark

Boston

Witham

East Retford

Worksop

Mansfield

Sutton-in-Ashfield

Heanor

Ilkeston

Nottingham

Beeston

Long Eaton

Burton-on-Trent

Ashby-de-la-Zouch

Derby

Uttoxeter

Leek

Buxton

Matlock

Chesterfield

Sheffield

Rotherham

Barnsley

Doncaster

Scunthorpe

Grimsby

Cleethorpes

Immingham

Barton-upon-Humber

Goole

Selby

Pontefract

Wakefield

Dewsbury

Huddersfield

Halifax

Bradford

Leeds

Harrogate

Knaresborough

Ripon

York

Beverley

Hull

Withernsea

Hornsea

Bridlington

Filey

Scarborough

Whitby

Redcar

Middlesbrough

Teesside

Hartlepool

Stockton

Billingham

Darlington

Bishop Auckland

Barnard Castle

Richmond

Northallerton

Thirsk

Pickering

Malton

Driffield

Flamborough Hd.

Spurn Hd.

Consett

Durham

Newcastle

Gateshead

Tynemouth

South Shields

Sunderland

Houghton-le-Spring

Peterlee

Washington

Blyth

Ashington

Morpeth

Alnwick

Coquet

Amble

Berwick-upon-Tweed

Holy I.

Farne Is.

Bamburgh

Eyemouth

St. Abb's Hd.

Dunbar

Haddington

Musselburgh

Edinburgh

Leith

Linlithgow

Bathgate

Falkirk

Stirling

Alloa

Dunfermline

Kirkcaldy

Kinross

L. Leven

Anstruther

Fife Ness

North Berwick

Bass Rock

Kelso

Coldstream

Jedburgh

Galashiels

Selkirk

Peebles

Moorfoot Hills

Lammermuir Hills

Pentland Hills

Hawick

Langholm

Carlisle

Gretna Green

Annan

Dumfries

Lockerbie

Moffat

Leadhills

Lanark

Carstairs

Biggar

Sanquhar

Nith

New Galloway

Newton Stewart

Castle Douglas

Dalbeattie

Kirkcudbright

Solway Firth

Maryport

Workington

Whitehaven

St. Bee's Hd.

Keswick

Derwent

Cockermouth

Derwentwater

Seascale

Millom

Barrow

Walney I.

Ulverston

Ambleside

Windermere

Kendal

Morecambe

Heysham

Fleetwood

Cleveleys

Blackpool

Lytham-St. Annes

Preston

Southport

Formby Pt.

Ormskirk

Bootle

Liverpool

Birkenhead

Wallasey

Widnes

Runcorn

St. Helens

Wigan

Bolton

Bury

Rochdale

Oldham

Manchester

Salford

Stockport

Ashton-under-Lyne

Stalybridge

Hyde

Sale

Altrincham

Warrington

Northwich

Winsford

Crewe

Nantwich

Whitchurch

Market Drayton

Newcastle-under-Lyne

Stoke-on-Trent

Congleton

Macclesfield

Knutsford

Glossop

Lancaster

Forest of Bowland

Ingleborough

Settle

Skipton

Keighley

Colne

Nelson

Burnley

Accrington

Blackburn

Darwen

Chorley

Leyland

Clitheroe

Pen-y-Ghent 693

Whernside 737

Ingleton

Wensleydale

Swaledale

Ure

Nidd

Wharfe

Aire

Ribble

Hebden Bridge

Todmorden

Rhyl

Prestatyn

Colwyn Bay

Llandudno

Conwy

Bangor

Caernarfon

Menai Strait

Beaumaris

Amlwch

Holyhead

Holy I.

Skerries

Bardsey I.

Pwllheli

Porthmadog

Blaenau Ffestiniog

Harlech

Barmouth

Dolgellau

Bala

Llangollen

Wrexham

Flint

Mold

Denbigh

Ruthin

St. Asaph

Corwen

Oswestry

Wem

Bangor

Belfast

Belfast Lough

Newtownards

Strangford L.

Larne

Downpatrick

Donaghadee

Portpatrick

Stranraer

North Channel

Portrush

I. Magee

Ayr

Girvan

Ailsa Craig

Maybole

Prestwick

Kilmarnock

Irvine

Saltcoats

Largs

Ardrossan

Dumbarton

Clydebank

Glasgow

Paisley

Port Glasgow

Greenock

Helensburgh

Rutherglen

Hamilton

Motherwell

Wishaw

Coatbridge

Airdrie

Firth of Clyde

Arran

Goat Fell 874

Campbeltown

Mull of Kintyre

Gigha I.

Jura

Sound of Jura

Crinan

Lochgilphead

Inveraray

L. Fyne

Ochil Hills

Forth

L. Lomond

Ben Lomond 974

L. Katrine

Trossachs

Wigtown

Wigtown Bay

Whithorn

Luce Bay

Mull of Galloway

Galloway

Kintyre

Merrick 843

Doon

Ayr

Pt. of Ayre

Ramsey

Douglas

Castletown

Port Erin

Calf of Man

Peel

Eden

Penrith

Alston

Appleby

Ullswater

HADRIAN'S WALL

S. Tyne

N. Tyne

Hexham

Blaydon

Wallsend

Tyne

Wear

Tees

Swale

Lune

Tweed

Till

Broad Law 840

The Cheviot 816

Flodden

Coldstream

Silloth

Wasdale

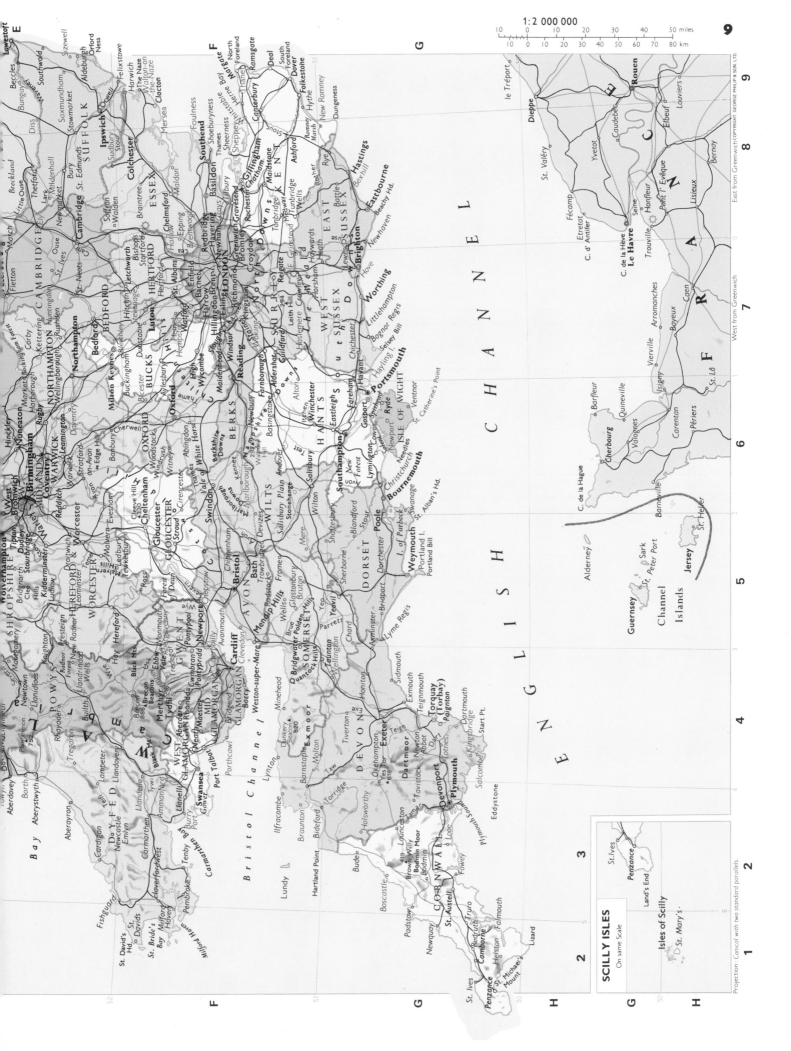

1:2 000 000

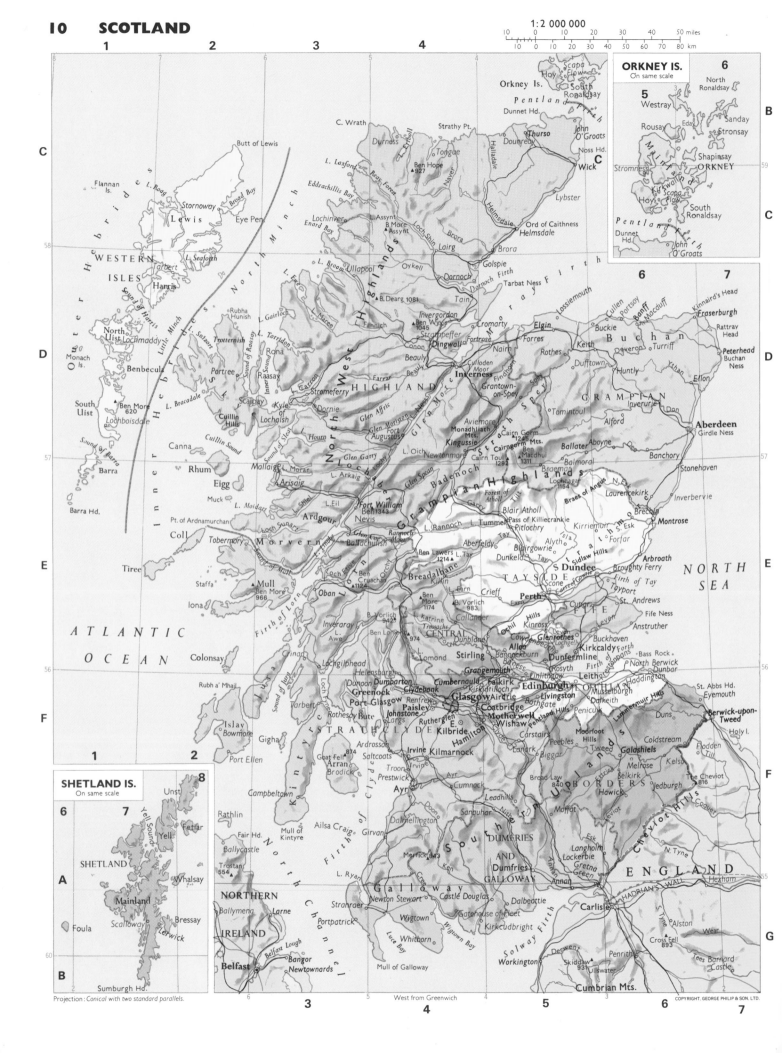

ORKNEY IS.
On same scale

SHETLAND IS.
On same scale

Projection: Conical with two standard parallels.

West from Greenwich

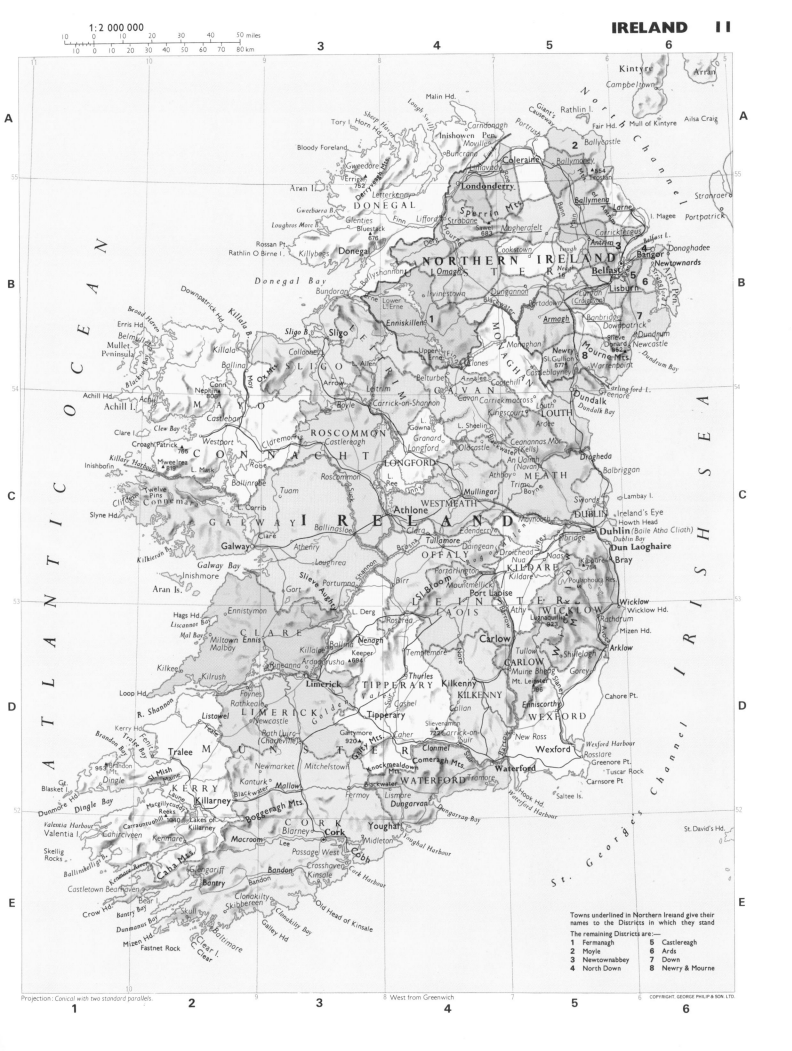

1:2 000 000

10   0   10   20   30   40   50 miles
10   0 10 20 30 40 50 60 70 80 km

Towns underlined in Northern Ireland give their
names to the Districts in which they stand
The remaining Districts are:—

1	Fermanagh	5	Castlereagh
2	Moyle	6	Ards
3	Newtownabbey	7	Down
4	North Down	8	Newry & Mourne

Projection: Conical with two standard parallels.

West from Greenwich

COPYRIGHT. GEORGE PHILIP & SON. LTD.

1:5 000 000

20 10 0   40   60   80   100 miles
40   20 0   40   120   160 km

FRENCH DEPARTMENTS

A.	Ai.	01 Ain
	Ai.	02 Aisne
	Al.	03 Allier
	H.A.	04 Hautes-Alpes
	A.M.	05 Alpes-Maritimes
	Ar.	06 Ardèche
	Ar.	07 Ardèche
	Ard.	08 Ardennes
	Ar.	09 Ariège
	Aub.	10 Aube
	Aud.	11 Aude
	Av.	12 Aveyron
	B.Rh.	13 Bouches-du-Rhône
	Ca.	14 Calvados
	Ca.	15 Cantal
	Ch.M.	16 Charente
	Che.	17 Charente-Maritime
	Che.	18 Cher
	Co.	19 Corrèze
	C.O.	20 a) Haute-Corse b) Corse du Sud
	C.O.	21 Côte-d'Or
	Co.	22 Côtes d'Armor
	Cr.	23 Creuse
	D.	24 Dordogne
	Do.	25 Doubs
	Dr.	26 Drôme
	E.	27 Eure
	E.L.	28 Eure-et-Loir
	F.	29 Finistère
	G.	30 Gard
	H.G.	31 Haute-Garonne
	Gi.	32 Gers
	Gi.	33 Gironde
	H.V.	34 Hérault
	I.V.	35 Ille-et-Vilaine
	I.	36 Indre
	I.L.	37 Indre-et-Loire
	Is.	38 Isère
	Ju.	39 Jura
	L.	40 Landes
	L.C.	41 Loir-et-Cher
	Lo.	42 Loire
	H.L.	43 Haute-Loire
	L.A.	44 Loire-Atlantique
	Loi.	45 Loiret
	Lo.	46 Lot
	Loz.	47 Lot-et-Garonne
	Loz.	48 Lozère
	M.L.	49 Maine-et-Loire
	Ma.	50 Manche
	Ma.	51 Marne
	H.M.	52 Haute-Marne
	May.	53 Mayenne
	M.M.	54 Meurthe-et-Moselle
	Me.	55 Meuse
	Mo.	56 Morbihan
	Mo.	57 Moselle
	N.	58 Nièvre
	N.	59 Nord
	O.	60 Oise
	Or.	61 Orne
	P.C.	62 Pas-de-Calais
	P.D.	63 Puy-de-Dôme
	P.A.	64 Pyrénées-Atlantiques
	H.P.	65 Hautes-Pyrénées
	P.O.	66 Pyrénées-Orientales
	B.R.	67 Bas Rhin
	H.R.	68 Haut Rhin
	Rh.	69 Rhône
	H.S.	70 Haute-Saône
	S.L.	71 Saône-et-Loire
	Sa.	72 Sarthe
	Sa.	73 Savoie
	H.Sa.	74 Haute-Savoie
	S.Me.	75 Paris
	S.M.	76 Seine-Maritime
	S.M.	77 Seine-et-Marne
	Yv.	78 Yvelines
	D.S.	79 Deux-Sèvres
	So.	80 Somme
	T.	81 Tarn
	T.G.	82 Tarn-et-Garonne
	Va.	83 Var
	V.	84 Vaucluse
	Ve.	85 Vendée
	Vi.	86 Vienne
	H.V.	87 Haute-Vienne
	Vo.	88 Vosges
	Y.	89 Yonne
	Bel.	90 Belfort
	Es.	91 Essonne
	H.Se.	92 Hauts-Seine
	S.Se-D.	93 Seine-St-Denis
	V.M.	94 Val-de-Marne
	V.O.	95 Val-d'Oise

CORSICA
On same scale

Corse

Haute-Corse
Mte. Rotondo 2625
Corse du Sud

ENGLISH CHANNEL

BAY OF BISCAY

MEDITERRANEAN SEA

GERMANY

BELGIUM

SWITZERLAND

ITALY

Projection: Conical with two standard parallels

East from Greenwich
West from Greenwich

1:5 000 000

50 0 50 100 miles
50 0 50 100 150 km

East from Greenwich
West from Greenwich

Projection : Conical with two standard parallels

FRANCE

Montpellier · Béziers · Narbonne · Perpignan · Toulouse
Golfe du Lion · Can. du Midi · Carcassonne · Foix
Bayonne · Biarritz · Pau · Lourdes · Tarbes
Bay of Biscay · San Sebastián · Pamplona

PYRÉNÉES · ANDORRA · 3404

Gerona · Colonia · Badalona · BARCELONA · Sabadell · Tarrasa · Hospitalet
Tarragona · Lérida · Huesca · Manresa · Vich

ARAGÓN · Zaragoza · NAVARRA · Logroño · Vitoria · Bilbao · Baracaldo
PAÍS VASCO · CANTÁBRICA · Oviedo · Gijón · 2926

GALICIA · La Coruña · El Ferrol · Santiago de Compostela · Lugo · Pontevedra · Vigo · Orense
C. Ortegal · C. Finisterre

ASTURIAS · LEÓN · CASTILLA Y LEÓN · Burgos · Palencia · Valladolid · Zamora · Salamanca · Ávila · Segovia
Sierra de la Demanda · LA RIOJA

MADRID · Getafe · Leganés · Alcalá de Henares · Guadalajara · Soria
CASTILLA LA MANCHA · Toledo · Montes de Toledo · Cuenca · Serranía de Cuenca · Albacete · Ciudad Real

SPAIN · EXTREMADURA · Cáceres · Badajoz · Mérida · SIERRA MORENA

PORTUGAL · Porto · Coimbra · Lisboa · Setúbal · Évora · Santarém · Braga
MINHO · DOURO LITORAL · TRÁS OS MONTES · BEIRA ALTA · BEIRA BAIXA · BEIRA LITORAL
ESTREMADURA · RIBATEJO · ALTO ALENTEJO · BAIXO ALENTEJO · ALGARVE
C. de S. Vicente · Lagos · Faro

VALENCIA · Castellón de la Plana · Golfo de Valencia · Albufera de Valencia
MURCIA · Alicante · Elche · Murcia · Lorca · Cartagena · Mar Menor

ANDALUCÍA · Sevilla · Córdoba · Jaén · Linares · Granada · Sa. Nevada · 3478 Mulhacén
Málaga · Marbella · Algeciras · La Línea de la Concepción · Gibraltar (Br.)
Jerez · Cádiz · Huelva · Almería · Guadix
Golfo de Cádiz · Strait of Gibraltar · Ceuta (Sp.) · Tánger · Tetouan

MOROCCO

ISLAS BALEARES · Mallorca · Palma · Menorca · Mahón · Ibiza · Formentera · Cabrera

MEDITERRANEAN SEA

ATLANTIC OCEAN

ALGERIA · Alger · Blida · Oran · Mostaganem · Ech Chelf · Koléa · Boufarik

Lyon
FRANCE
Grenoble
Mt. Pelvoux 4103
Briançon
Valence
Montelimar
DAUPHINÉ
Nyons
Orange
Avignon
PROVENCE
Aix
Marseille
Toulon
Îles d'Hyères

SWITZERLAND
Genève
Thonon
Martigny
Matterhorn Mte. Rosa
Mt. Blanc 4807
V. D'AOSTA
Aosta
Gran Paradiso
Col du Pt. St-Bernard
Susa
PIEMONTE
Pinerolo
Mt. Viso 3841
Saluzzo
Cúneo
Mondovi
Tende
MONACO
Nice
Cannes
Côte d'Azur
San Remo
Imperia
Riv. di Ponente
Savona
Li Giovi
Génova (Genoa)

Passo del S. Gottardo 2108
Domodóssola
Lago Maggiore
Locarno
Lugano
Como
L. di Como
Lecco
Bérgamo
Busto Arsizio
LOMBARDIA
Milano (Milan)
Monza
Brescia
Novara
Vercelli
Pavia
Torino (Turin)
Chivasso
Casale
Asti
Alessándria
Alba
Piacenza
Cremona
Adda
Parma
Réggio
Módena
Bologna
EMILIA ROMAGNA
Mte. Cimone 2165
Carrara
La Spézia
Riv. di Levante
Chiávari

Brenner 1371
Merano
Bressanone
Bolzano
TRENTINO ALTO-ADIGE
Ortles 3899
Adamello 3554
Trento
Rovereto
Schio
Vicenza
Verona
Mántova (Mantua)
Adige
Roviga
Ferrara
Comácchio
Ravenna
Forlì
Cesena
Rimini

Villach
Klagenfurt
Karawanken
Triglav 2863
Kobarid (Caporetto)
Údine
FRIULI VENEZIA GIULIA
Gorizia
Trieste
SLOVENIA
Ljubljana
Zagreb
Istra
Rijeka (Fiume)
CROA
Pula (Pola)
Krk
Cres
Lošinj
Pag
Zadar
Dugi Otok
Šibenik
Split
Brač
Hvar
Korčula
Lastovo
Vis

Bleiburg
Maribor
Nagykanizsa
Varaždin
Sava
Bjelovar
Karlovac
Sisak
Novsk
Velika Kapela
Bihać
Banja Luka
BOS
HERZI
Dinara 1913
Troglav

ADRIATIC SEA

LIGURIAN SEA
C. Corse
Capraia
Piombino
Portoferráio
Elba
Calvi
Bastia
Mt. Cinto 2710
CORSE (CORSICA) (Fr.)
Aléria
Ajaccio
Sartène
Pto. Vecchio
Bonifacio
Bouches de Bonifacio
Maddalena
Caprera
Olbia (Terranova)
Golfo Aranci

Pisa
Livorno (Leghorn)
Lucca
Pistóia
Prato
Firenze (Florence)
TOSCANA
Siena
Arezzo
Cortona
Volterra
Arno
L. Trasimeno
Pontedera
Orbetello
Mte. Argentario
Fiora
Civitavecchia
Grosseto
Amiata 1738
L. di Bolsena
Orvieto
Viterbo
L. di Bracciano
Lido di Óstia
ROMA (Rome)
Velletri
Ánzio
Latina
Frosinone
Sabáudia
Terracina
Fondi
Gaeta
Garigliano
Volturna
Ísole Ponziane
Íschia

Chiusi
PERÚGIA
Assisi
Spoleto 2478
UMBRIA
Foligno
Monti Vettore
Téramo
Gran Sasso 2914
L'Aquila
ABRUZZI
Mt. Amaro 2795
Rieti
Terni
Tíber

Macerata
Civitanova
San Benedetto
Ascoli Piceno
Pescara
Ortona
Chieti
Lanciano
Vasto
Térmoli

Loreto
Senigállia
Ancona
Fabriano
Urbíno
Pésaro
Fano
SAN MARINO

Sannicandro
Monte S. Ángelo
Monte Gargano
G. di Manfredónia
Fóggia
Cerignola
MOLISE
Campobasso
S. Severo
1056
Barletta
Trani
Andria
Corato
Molfetta
Bari
Spinazzola
Monópoli
Putignano
Matera
TARANTO
BASILICATA
Benevento
Caserta
Aversa
Napoli (Naples)
Vesuvio 1277
Torre del Greco
Nocera
Avellino
Éboli
Salerno
Sele
Castellammare
Sorrento
Cápri
Potenza
Agri
Eclano
Pisciotta
Sinni
2271
Golfo di Táranto

2855
Asinara
C. Falcone
Golfo dell' Asinara
Porto Torres
Álghero
Bosa
Nuoro
SARDEGNA (SARDINIA)
Oristano
Sórgono
Mt. Gennargentu 1834
Arbatax
Tortolì
Golfo di Oristano
Terralba
Iglésias
Carbonia
Portoscuso
G. di Pálmas
Cágliari
Golfo di Cágliari
C. Carbonara
C. Spartivento
Sássari
C. Mte. Santo

TYRRHENIAN SEA
3719

Cosenza
1929
Nicastro
CALABRIA
Crotone
Catanzaro
Sambiase
Pizzo
Palmi
Tauriánova
Réggio
C. Spartivento
Str. di Messina
Corigliano

Ústica (It.)
Isole Eólie o Lípari
Strómboli
Salina
Vulcano
Lípari
C. Peloro
Messina
Milazzo
Patti

Isole Egadi
Trápani
Érice
Castellammare
Palermo
Términi
Cefalù
Alcamo
Ségesta
Favignana
Marsala
Castelvetrano
Selinunte
Menfi
Sciacca
Pto. Empédocle
Agrigento
Platani
Favara
Caltagirone
Caltanissetta
Enna
Monti Nebrodi
Adrano
Etna 3340
Giarre
Paternò
Léntini
Augusta
Catánia
Mistretta
Ferla
Gela
Licata
Salso
Ragusa
Módica
Vittória
Noto
Ispica
Siracusa (Syracuse)
C. Passero

MEDITE

1730

Binzert (Bizerte)
Annaba
Béja
Tunis
TUNISIA
G. de Tunis
C. Bon
Nabeul
Skikda
C. de Fer
La Galite
Constantine
ALGERIA
Khenchela
Tébessa
Kairouan
Sousse
G. de Hammamet

Pantelleria (Ital.)

Lampedusa (Ital.)

Gozo
Comino
Valletta
Mdina
MALTA

RUSSIA
1. Daghestan Rep.
2. Kabardino–Balkar Rep.
3. Mari Rep.
4. Mordovian Rep.
5. North Ossetian Rep.
6. Tatar Rep.
7. Udmurt Rep.
8. Chuvash Rep.
9. Checheno–Ingush Rep.
AZERBAIJAN
10. Nakhichevan Rep.
GEORGIA
11. Abkhaz Rep.
12. Adzhar Rep.

Projection: Conical Orthomorphic with two standard parallels

East from Greenwich

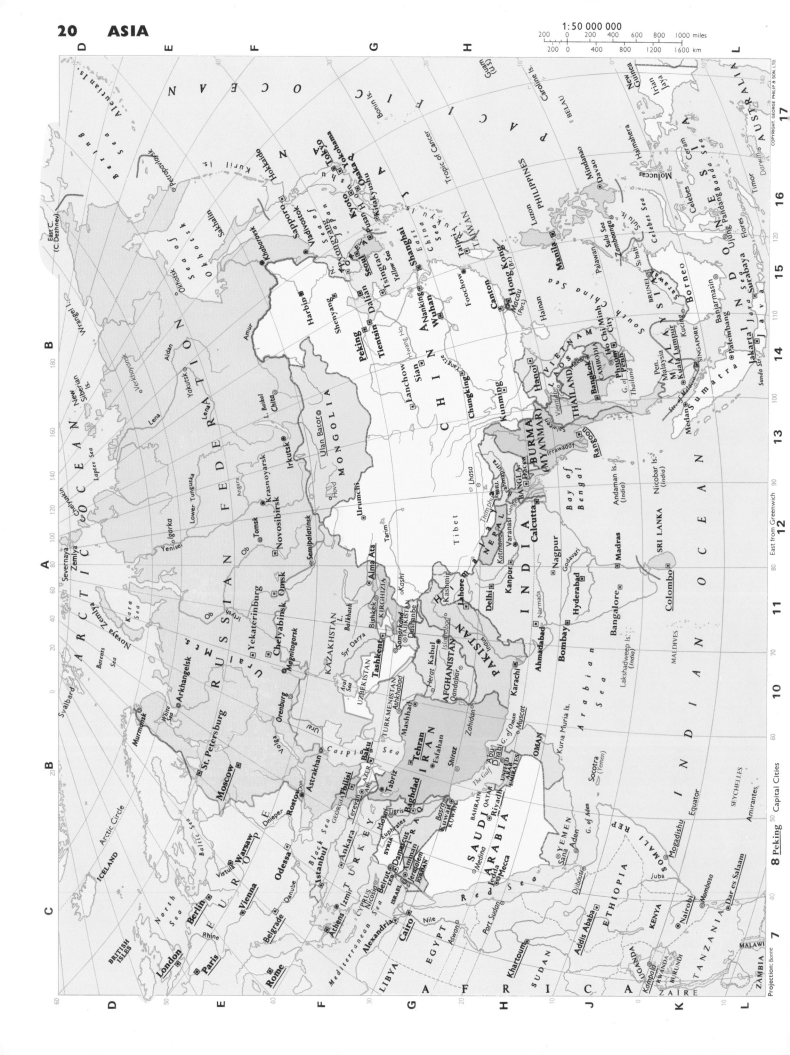

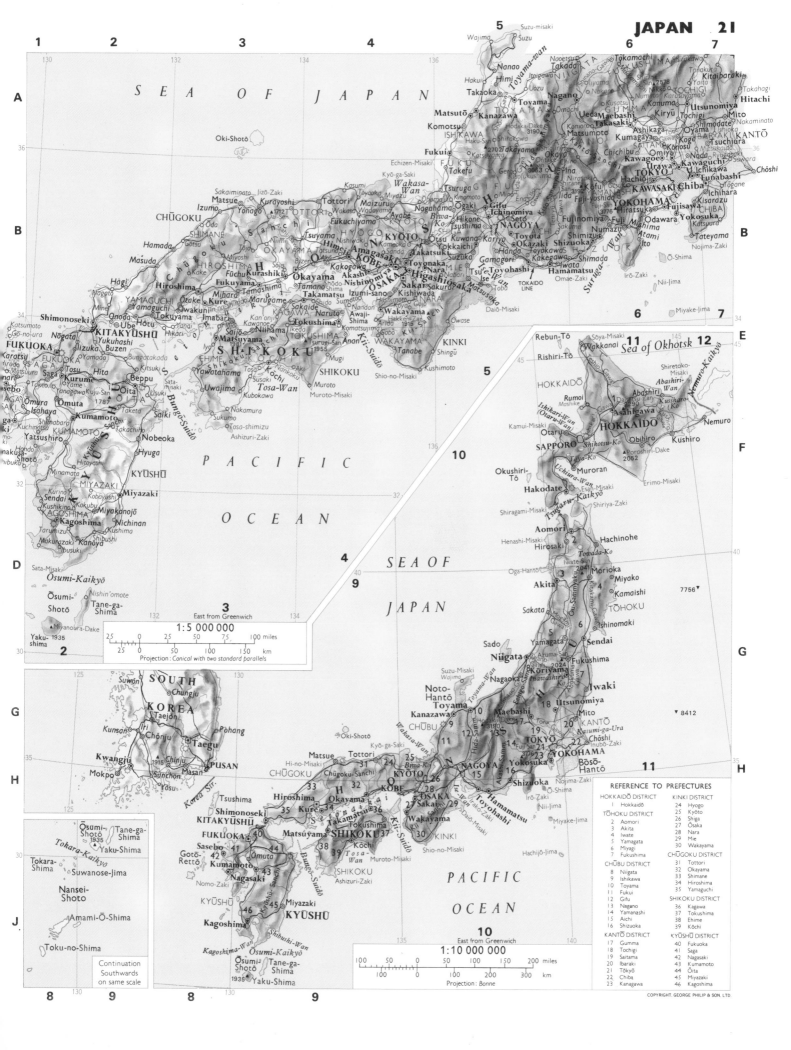

1:20 000 000

100   0   100   200   300   400 miles
100   0 100 200 300 400 500 600 km

JAPAN

EAST CHINA SEA

Ryūkyū-Rettō

Okinawa 7507

Sakishima-Guntō

Tropic of Cancer

SOUTH KOREA

NORTH KOREA

Fukuoka
Nagasaki
Sasebo
Pusan
Taegu
Kwangju
Mokpo
Cheju
Cheju Do 1950

Pyongyang
Inch'on
Seoul
Taejon

YELLOW SEA

DALIAN
QINGDAO
Yantai
Weifang
Qinhuangdao

SHENYANG
HARBIN
Qiqihar
Changchun
Jilin
Fushun
Benxi
Anshan
Liaoyang

BEIJING
TIANJIN (Tientsin)
Baoding
Tangshan
Zhangjiakou
Datong

TAIYUAN
Shijiazhuang
Handan

SHANGHAI
NANJING
Hangzhou
Ningbo
Wenzhou
Wuxi
Suzhou
Shaoxing

JIANGSU
ZHEJIANG
ANHUI

SHANDONG
Jinan
Zibo
Xuzhou

HENAN
Zhengzhou
Kaifeng
Luoyang
Nanyang

XI'AN
Baoji

WUHAN
Changsha
Nanchang
Hengyang

JIANGXI
HUNAN
HUBEI
FUJIAN

Fuzhou
Xiamen
Quanzhou

TAIWAN (FORMOSA)
Taibei (Taipei)
Gaoxiong
Tainan
Jilong

CHONGQING
CHENGDU
GUIZHOU
Guiyang
SICHUAN
Zigong
Neijiang

GUANGZHOU (Canton)
GUANGDONG
Foshan
Shantou
Zhanjiang
Macao
Hong Kong
Kowloon
HAINAN
Haikou
Hainan Dao

SOUTH CHINA SEA

PHILIPPINES
Luzon

Bushi Channel
Batan Is.

GUANGXI
Liuzhou
Guilin
Nanning

Kunming
YUNNAN

VIETNAM
HANOI
Haiphong

LAOS
THAILAND

BURMA (MYANMAR)
Mandalay
Myitkyina

XIZANG (TIBET)
Lhasa
Nyainqêntanglha Shan
Tanggula Shan

QINGHAI
Xining
Golmud
Bayan Har Shan

Kunlun Shan
Altun Shan

GANSU
Lanzhou
Yinchuan

NINGXIA
Wuhai

INNER MONGOLIA (NEI MONGGOL)
BAOTOU
Hohhot

MONGOLIA
Ulaanbaatar (Ulan Bator)
Hangayn Nuruu
Henтiyn Nuruu

RUSSIA
Irkutsk
Ulan Ude
Chita
Khabarovsk
Blagoveshchensk
Vladivostok
Ussuriysk

Amur

XINJIANG UYGUR
Ürümqi (Urumchi)
Tarim Pendi
Dzungaria (Junggar Pendi)
Tian Shan
Kashi
Aksu
Hotan
Turpan (Turfan)
Hami

Tarim

Bosten Hu
Lop Nur

KAZAKHSTAN
Karaganda
Semipalatinsk
Alma Ata
Ozero Balkhash

KIRGHIZIA
Bishkek

JAMMU & KASHMIR
Karakoram

NEPAL
Kathmandu
Mt. Everest 8848

BHUTAN
Thimphu

BANGLADESH
Dhaka
Chittagong

INDIA
CALCUTTA
Kanpur
Lucknow
Varanasi
Allahabad
Patna
Ranchi
Jamshedpur
Cuttack

ASSAM
Gauhati

BAY OF BENGAL

East from Greenwich

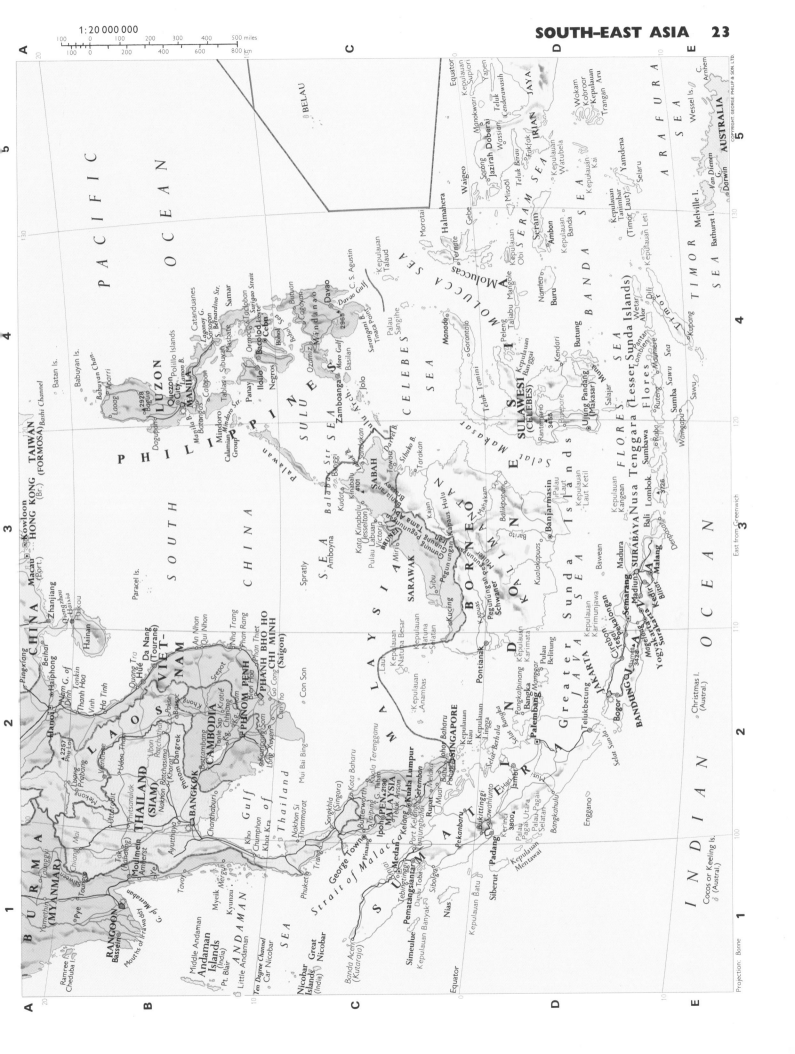

1:20 000 000

PACIFIC OCEAN

SOUTH CHINA SEA

CHINA

TAIWAN (FORMOSA)

HONG KONG (Br.)

Macau (Port.)

Hainan

Paracel Is.

VIET-NAM

LAOS

THAILAND (SIAM)

BANGKOK

CAMBODIA

PHNOM PENH

PHANH BHO HO CHI MINH (Saigon)

BURMA (MYANMAR)

RANGOON

Gulf of Thailand

ANDAMAN SEA

Andaman Islands (India)

Nicobar Islands (India)

BELAU

PHILIPPINES

LUZON

MANILA

Quezon City

Mindoro

Panay

Negros

Cebu

Bacolod

Iloilo

Mindanao

Davao

SULU SEA

Zamboanga

CELEBES SEA

MALAYSIA

SINGAPORE

Kuala Lumpur

SARAWAK

SABAH

BRUNEI

BORNEO (KALIMANTAN)

Banjarmasin

Pontianak

Balikpapan

SULAWESI (CELEBES)

Ujung Pandang (Makasar)

MOLUCCA SEA

BANDA SEA

SERAM SEA

IRIAN JAYA

ARAFURA SEA

CELEBES SEA

SUMATERA

Palembang

Padang

Medan

Bukittinggi

JAVA SEA

FLORES SEA

Lesser Sunda Islands (Nusa Tenggara)

TIMOR SEA

INDONESIA

JAKARTA

BANDUNG

SURABAYA

SEMARANG

Greater Sunda Islands

INDIAN OCEAN

Christmas I. (Austral.)

Cocos or Keeling Is. (Austral.)

AUSTRALIA

Darwin

Equator

East from Greenwich

Projection: Bonne

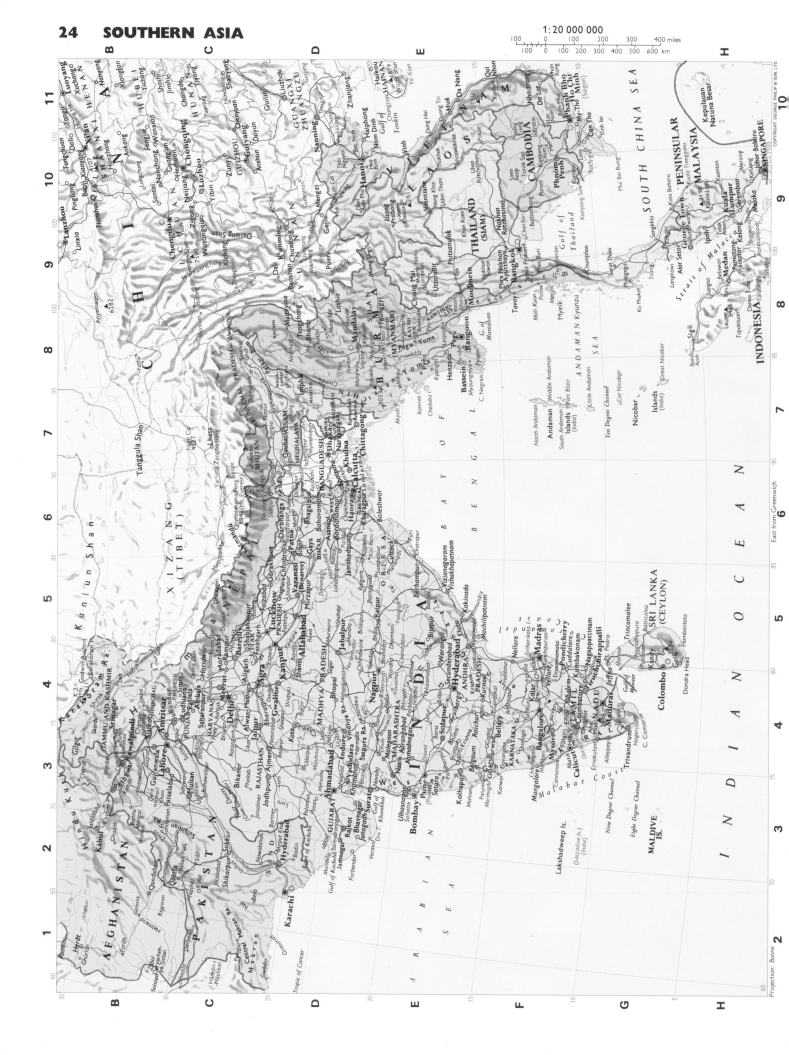

1:20 000 000

COPYRIGHT GEORGE PHILIP & SON, LTD.

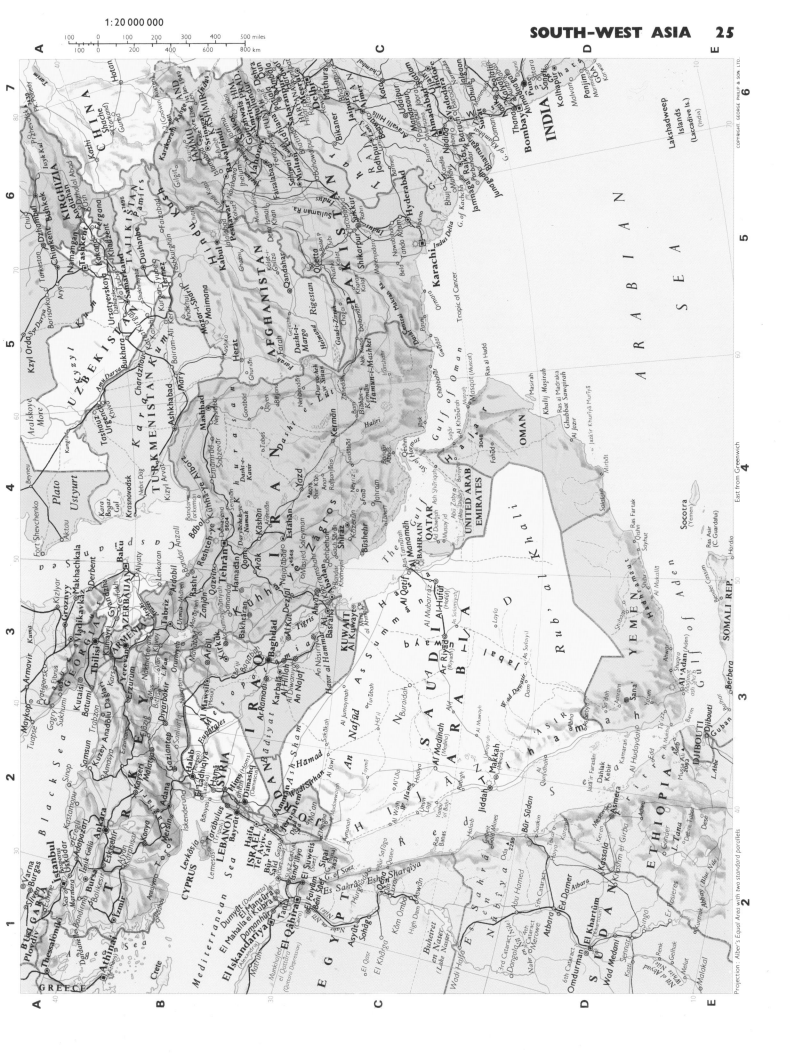

1:20 000 000

100   0   100   200   300   400   500 miles
100   0   200   400   600   800 km

Projection: Alber's Equal Area with two standard parallels

A   B   C   D   E

CHINA
KIRGHIZIA
UZBEKISTAN
TAJIKISTAN
TURKMENISTAN
AFGHANISTAN
PAKISTAN
INDIA
GOA
Lakshadweep Islands (Laccadive Is.) (India)

ARABIAN SEA

IRAN
Tehrān
Mashhad
Herat
Kabul
Kandahar
Quetta
Karachi
Bombay
Hyderabad
Delhi
Jaipur
Ahmadabad

GEORGIA
ARMENIA
AZERBAIJAN
Baku
Tbilisi
Yerevan

Black Sea
TURKEY
Ankara
Istanbul
Izmir
Adana
CYPRUS
SYRIA
LEBANON
Beyrouth
ISRAEL
Tel Aviv
JORDAN
'Ammān
Damascq (Damascus)
Halab (Aleppo)
Dimashq

Mediterranean Sea
GREECE
Crete

IRAQ
Baghdad
Basrah
Al Mawsil (Mosul)
Kirkūk

KUWAIT
Al Kuwayt
BAHRAIN
Al Manāmah
QATAR
Ad Dawḥah
UNITED ARAB EMIRATES
Abū Zaby
OMAN
Masqat (Muscat)
Gulf of Oman

SAUDI ARABIA
Ar Riyāḍ (Riyadh)
Al Madīnah (Medina)
Makkah (Mecca)
Jiddah
Al Hufūf

Rub' al Khali
An Nafūd
Persian Gulf
Tropic of Cancer

YEMEN
Sana
Aden
Al 'Adan (Aden)
Gulf of Aden
Socotra (Yemen)
SOMALI REP.

Red Sea

EGYPT
El Qâhira (Cairo)
El Iskandarîya (Alexandria)
Suez
Nile

SUDAN
El Khartûm
Omdurman
Port Sudan

ETHIOPIA
Asmera
Addis
DJIBOUTI

East from Greenwich

NORTH ATLANTIC

OCEAN

6578

Cabo de São Vicente

SPAIN
Cádiz · Málaga · Almería
Str. of Gibraltar · Gibraltar (Br.) · Sidi-Bel-Abbès · Oran · Mostaganem · Ech Cheliff · Alger (Algiers) · Harrach · Tizi-Ouzou · Bejaia · Skikda · Annaba · Tabarka
Tanger · Ceuta (Sp.) · Melilla · Ghazaouet · Mascara · Tiaret · Hauts Plateaux · Blida · 2308 · Constantine · Guelma
Larache · El Hoceima · Tétouan · Tlemcen · Saïda · Bou Saâda · Sétif · Batna · TUNISIA
Ksar el Kebir · Oujda · Mecheria · El Bayadh · Khenchela · Biskra
Kenitra (Port Lyautey) · Fès · Taza · El Aricha · Djelfa · Djelfa · Ouled-Djellal · Nefta · Chott el Djerid · Gabès
Salé · Rabat · Meknès · Laghouat · Touggourt · El Oued · Tozeur · Matmata
Casablanca · MOROCCO · Moyen Atlas · Figuig · Beni Ounif · Ghardaïa · Ouargla · Sinaw
El Jadida · Berrechid · Settat · Khouribga · Beni Mellal · Béchar · Hassi er Rmel · Hassi Messaoud · Ghudamis
Ras Beddouza · Safi · Haut Atlas · Ar Rachidya · 2235 · Abadla · El Golea · Hassi el Gassi · Dardu
Essaouira · Marrakech · Bou Arfa · Ig · Beni Abbès · Ft. Mac-Mahon · Hassi Inifel · Ohanet
Dj. Toubkal · Ouarzazate · Kerzaz · Timimoun · Ft. Miribel · Bordj Omar Driss
C. Rhir · 4165 · Anti Atlas · Charouine · ALGERIA · In Belbel · In Salah · Illizi
Agadir · Taroudannt · Dra · Mengoub · Plateau du Tademaït · Miliana · Aoulef el Arab · Bj.-Tarat · Sardales
Ifni · Tiznit · Bou Izakarn · Adrar · Zaouiet Reggane · Arak · Djanet
Tarfaya (Villa Bens) · Tindouf · Ste. Marie · Ouallene · Bj.-in-Eker · Idelès

Madeira (Port.) · Funchal · Pto. Santo

Islas Canarias (Sp.) · Lanzarote · Arrecife
La Palma · Tenerife · Fuerteventura · Puerto del Rosario
Gomera · Sta. Cruz · Gran Canaria · Las Palmas · C. Juby
Hierro · El Aiún · Semara

WESTERN SAHARA
Dakhla · Pta. Durnford · Fderik · Zouérate
C. Barbas · Bu Craa · Bir Mogrein · Chegga
C. Bojador · Aïn Ben Tili · Terhazza · Taoudenni · Tanezrouft · Poste Maurice Cortier (Bidon 5)
Nouâdhibou (Port Etienne) · Ras Nouâdhibou · La Güera · Atar · Ouadâne · El Djouf · Haggar · Tahat · 2918 · Tamanrasset
Char · Chinguetti · Adrar des Iforhas · Tessalit · Admer
Oujeft · MAURITANIA · Mabrouk · Aïr · Monts Tamgak (Azbine) · 1900
Akjoujt · Araouane · Iférouane · Aoudéras
Rachid · Tidjikja · Tichit · Bou Djébéha · Kidal · Agadez
NIGER
Nouakchott · Boutilimit · Moudjéria · Akreijit · Togba · Kerchoual · I-n-Gall
Mederdra · Aleg · Kiffa · Tâmchekket · Oualâta · Tombouctou · Bamba · Bourem · Ménaka
St. Louis · Podor · Bogué · Kaédi · Néma · Goundam · Diré · Gourma-Rharous · Gao
Louga · Dagana · MALI · Bâssikounou · Niafouké · Kabara · Ansongo
Tivaouane · Dahra · Linguère · Sélibabi · Yélimané · Nioro du Sahel · Nara · Hombori · Tahoua · Tanout
Thiès · Matam · Bakel · Kayes · Mourdiah · Sokolo · Douentza · Djibo · Famalé · Téra · Tillabéri · Madaoua · Gangara · Kellé
Dakar · SENEGAL · Kaffrine · Kolokâni · Sarro · Mopti · Dori · BURKINA · Niamey · Birni Nkonni · Zinder
Kaolack · Tambacounda · Bafoulabé · Ké-Macina · Bandiagara · Ouahigouya · FASO · Say · Dosso · Argungu · Maradi · Tessaoua · Kamaguenan · Nguru
GAMBIA · Gambia · Satadougou · Kita · Banamba · Ségou · Djenné · Tougan · Kaya · Tillabéri · Birnin-Kebbi · Gandi · Sokoto · Katsina · Hadejia
Banjul · Maka · Kéniéba · Koulikoro · Niger · Sarro · Djibo · Yako · Botou · Jega · Gusau · Funtua · Dangora · Kano · Azare
Sedhiou · GUINEA-BISSAU · Bafatá · Siguiri · Douna · Koutiala · Ouagadougou · Fada N'Gourma · Diapaga · Kende · Kontagora · Zaria · Potiskum
Ziguinchor · Kédougou · Bamako · Bougouni · Sikasso · Léo · Pama · Kandi · Shanga · Bena · Kaduna · Lere
Bissau · BISSAU · Fouta Djalon · Tougué · Dinguiraye · Bobo-Dioulasso · Diébougou · Gaoua · Tumu · Gambaga · Mango · Kainji · Nasarawa · Keffi · Bauchi · Pindiga
Bolama · Gaoual · Boké · Télimélé · Kouroussa · Kankan · Bamford · Sidéradougou · Diébougou · Wa · Babana · Kaiama · Minna · NIGERIA · Shendam
Arquipélago dos Bijagós · Victoria · Kindia · Dabola · Faranah · Fabala · Odienné · Kong · Bouna · Sayelugu · Kintampo · Nikki · Parakou · Jebba · Ilorin · Bida · Kabba
C. Verga · GUINEA · Dubréka · Forécariah · 1948 · Kissidougou · Beyla · Macenta · Touba · Mankono · Katiola · Bondoukou · Wenchi · Salaga · BENIN · Shaki · Oyo · Oshogbo · Kabba · Makurdi · Wukari
Conakry · Kabala · Kenema · Man · Danane · Duékoué · Dabakala · Berekum · Yeji · TOGO · Ogbomosho · Iwa · Ife · Ado-Ekiti · Owo · Enugu · Gashaka
SIERRA LEONE · Makeni · Magburaka · Guéckédou · Odienné · IVORY COAST · Kumasi · Lake Volta · Abomey · Savalou · Ibadan · Abeokuta · Ondo · Benin City · Onitsha
Freetown · Yonibana · Bo · Kenema · Ganta · Séguéla · Bouaké · Bocanda · Biblara · GHANA · Nkawkaw · Kpalimé · Lagos · Akure · Sapele · Warri · CAMEROON
Waterloo · Moyamba · Danane · Daloa · Dimbokro · Yamoussoukro · Obuasi · Ho · Cotonou · Ijebu-Ode · Benin City · Port Harcourt · Buruku · Mont Cameroun 4070 · Douala
Sherbro · Bonthe · Sulima · LIBERIA · Guiglo · Gagnoa · Agboville · Dunkwa · Porto-Novo · Lomé · Aba · Calabar · Rey Malabo · Bioko
Monrovia · Marshall · Tapeta · Tai · Tiassalé · Prestea · Nsawam · Accra · Keta · Bight of Benin · Oktika · Limbe · Edéa
Buchanan · River Cess · Greenville · Garawe · Tabou · San-Pédro · Grand Lahou · Grand Bassam · Abidjan · Axim · Sekandi-Takoradi · Cape Coast · C. Three Points

20 · 15 · 10 · 5 · West from Greenwich · 0 · East from Greenwich · 5 · 10

ETHIOPIA

KENYA

TANZANIA

UGANDA

SUDAN

CENTRAL AFRICAN REPUBLIC

CHAD

NIGER

NIGERIA

CAMEROON

EQUATORIAL GUINEA

GABON

CONGO

ZAÏRE

RWANDA

BURUNDI

SHAMÂL KORDOFÂN

JANUB KORDOFÂN

BAHR EL GHAZAL

JANUB DARFÛR

SHAMÂL NÎL

AN NÎL EL AZRAQ (Blue Nile)

EN NÎL

JONGLEI

GHARB EL ISTIWÂ'IYA

SHARQ EL ISTIWÂ'IYA

EL BUHEIRAT

Addis Abeba

Asmera

KASSALA

Khartoum / El Khartûm

Omdurmân

El Obeid

Nairobi

Mombasa

Dar-es-Salaam

Zanzibar I.

Pemba I.

Mafia I.

Kampala

Kisangani

Kananga

Mbuji-Mayi

Kinshasa

Brazzaville

Bangui

N'djamena

Yaoundé

Douala

Libreville

Kano

Luanda

CABINDA

Mbini

Bata

L. Tana

L. Victoria

L. Tanganyika

L. Mobutu

L. Kyoga

L. Turkana (L. Rudolf)

Lac Tchad

Kilimanjaro 5895

Equator

CONGO

Zaïre

Kasai

Nile (Blue Nile)

Bahr el 'Arab

Chari

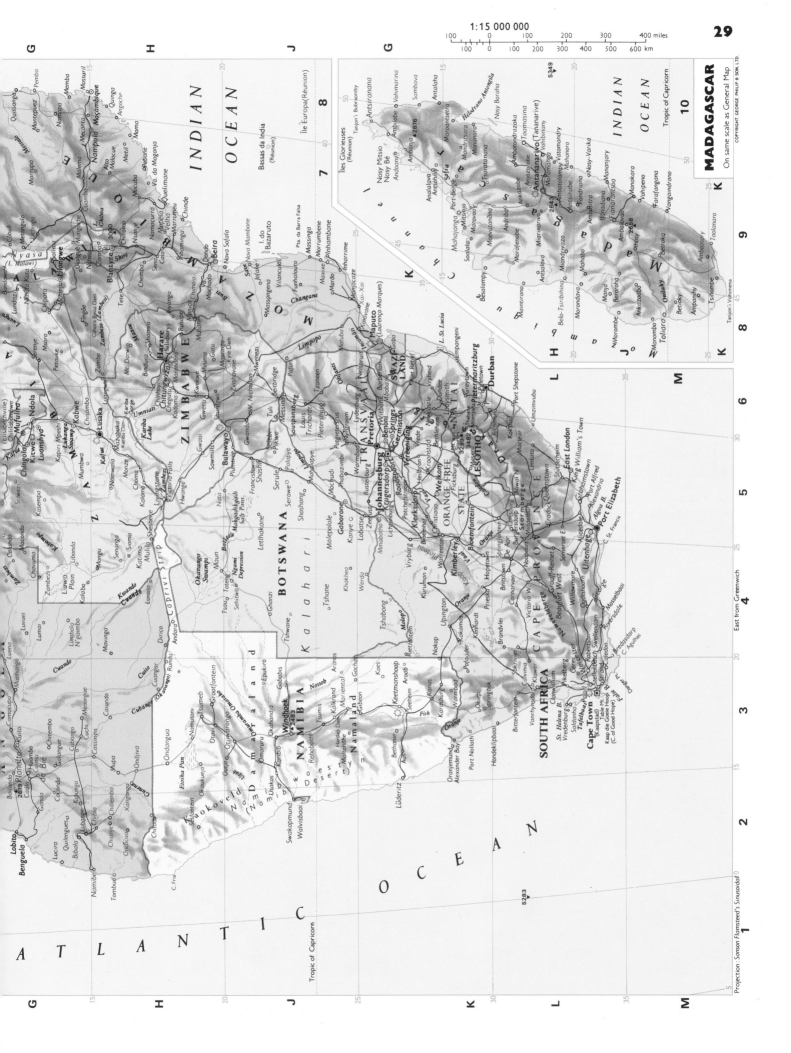

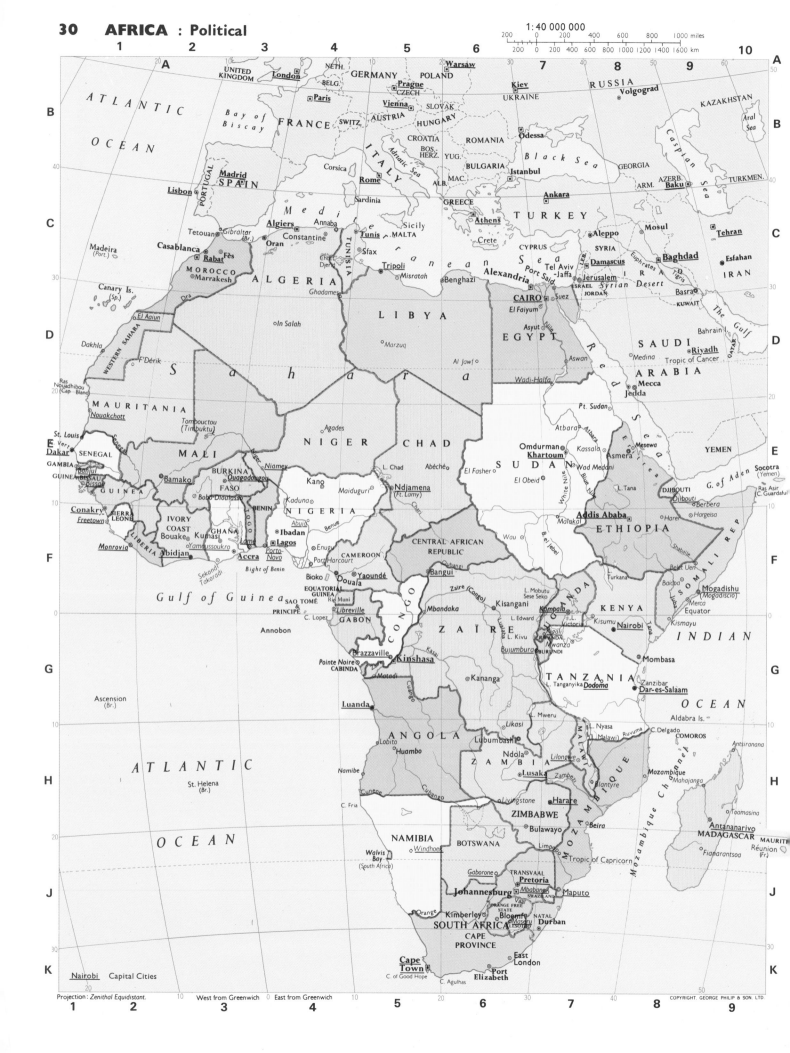

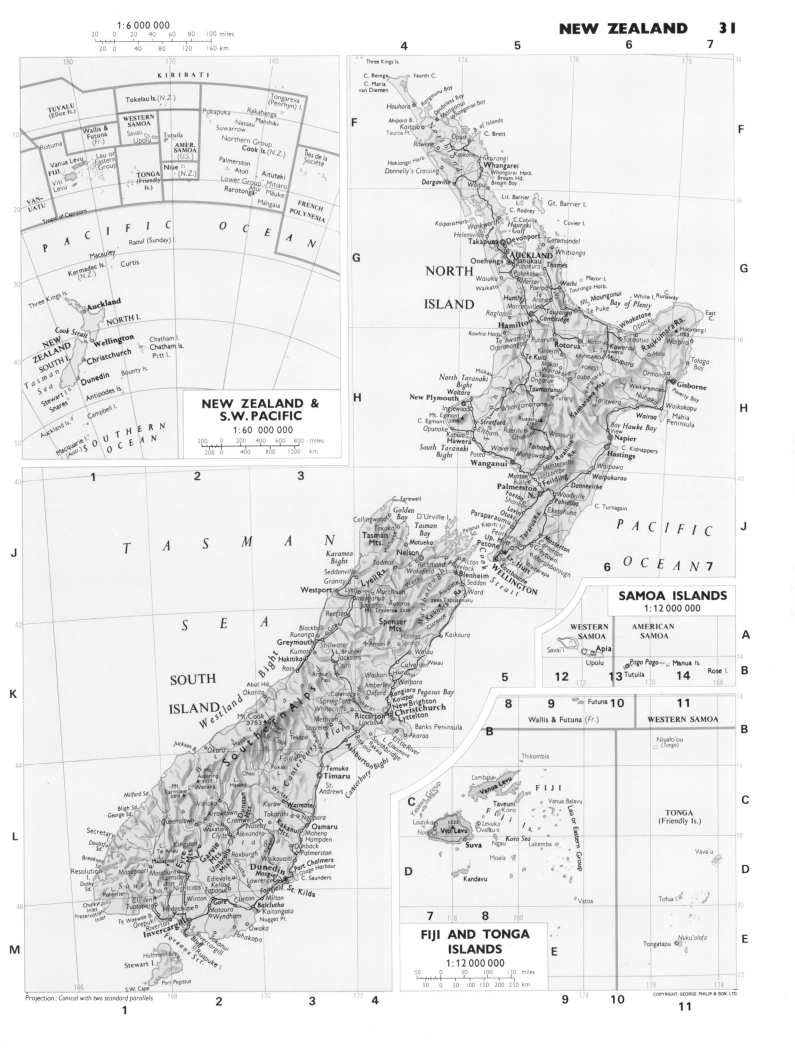

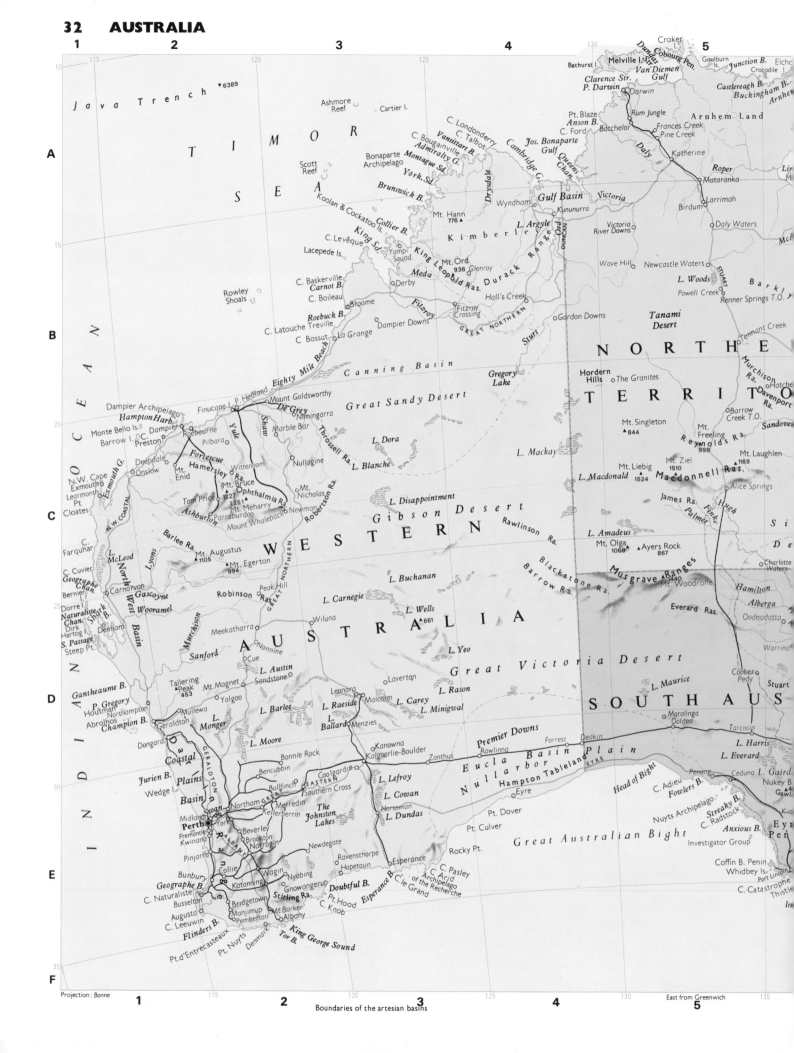

Boundaries of the artesian basins

East from Greenwich

1:12 000 000

AUSTRALASIA
PHYSICAL
1:80 000 000

TASMANIA

on same scale

COPYRIGHT. GEORGE PHILIP & SON. LTD.

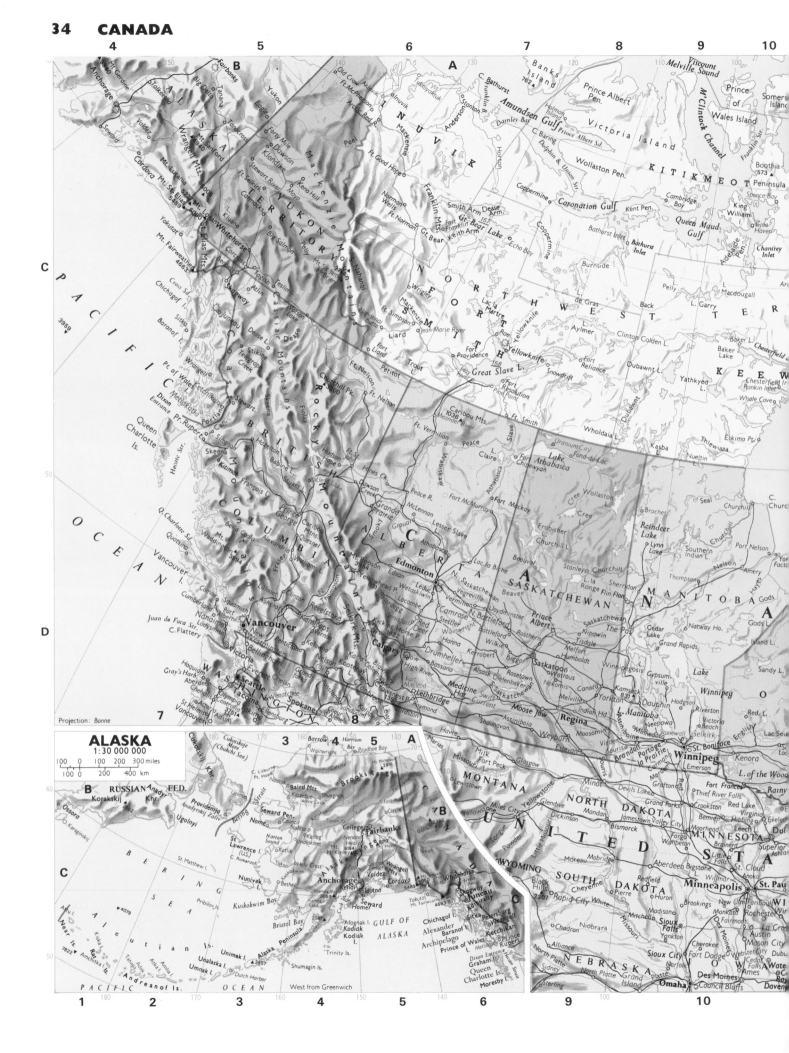

CANADA

BRITISH COLUMBIA   ALBERTA   SASKATCHEWAN   MANITOBA

Vancouver I.   Vancouver   Victoria   Bellingham   Everett   Seattle   Tacoma   Olympia

WASHINGTON   Spokane   Portland   Salem   Eugene

OREGON   IDAHO   Boise

MONTANA   Great Falls   Helena   Butte   Bozeman   Billings

NORTH DAKOTA   Bismarck

SOUTH DAKOTA   Pierre   Rapid City

WYOMING   Yellowstone National Park   Casper

NEBRASKA   North Platte

NEVADA   Reno   Carson City   Las Vegas

UTAH   Salt Lake City   Provo

COLORADO   Denver   Colorado Springs   Pueblo

KANSAS   Garden City   Dodge City

CALIFORNIA   Sacramento   San Francisco   Oakland   Berkeley   San Jose   Stockton   Modesto   Fresno   Bakersfield

LOS ANGELES   Long Beach   Anaheim   Santa Ana   Riverside   San Bernardino   San Diego   Tijuana   Mexicali

ARIZONA   Phoenix   Mesa   Tucson   Flagstaff   Grand Canyon Nat. Park

NEW MEXICO   Albuquerque   Santa Fe   Las Cruces   Roswell

OKLAHOMA   Amarillo   Lubbock

TEXAS   El Paso   Odessa   San Angelo   Abilene   Fort Worth   Austin   San Antonio

BAJA CALIFORNIA NORTE   BAJA CALIFORNIA SUR

SONORA   Hermosillo   Guaymas   Ciudad Obregón

CHIHUAHUA   Chihuahua   Ciudad Juárez

COAHUILA   Monclova   Monterrey   Nuevo Laredo   Torreón   Gómez Palacio

DURANGO   Los Mochis

MEXICO

PACIFIC OCEAN

West from Greenwich

HAWAII

Kauai   Niihau   Oahu   Honolulu   Pearl City   Molokai   Lanai   Maui   Kahoolawe   Hawaii   Hilo   Mauna Loa 4170   Haleakala 3056

PACIFIC OCEAN   Hawaiian Islands

HAWAII
1:10 000 000
20 0 20 40 60 80 miles
20 0 40 80 120 km

Projection: Albers' Equal Area with two standard parallels

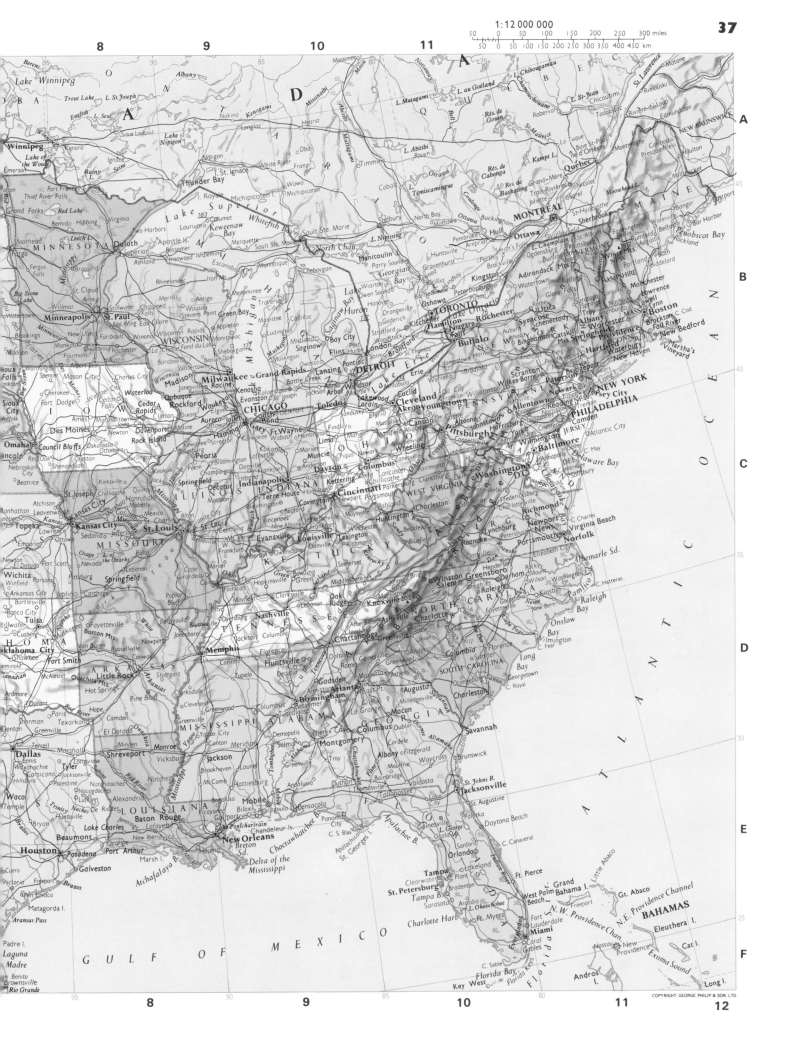

1 2 3 4 5 6 7

UNITED STATES

San Diego, Tijuana, Mexicali, Yuma, Phoenix, Tucson, Deming, Wichita Falls, Fort Worth, Dallas, Shreveport, Jackson, Birmingham, Meridian, Mont, Ensenada, Pta. Baja, Nogales, Bisbee, Ciudad Juárez, El Paso, Carlsbad, Abilene, Marshall, Monroe, Vicksburg, Pecos, S. Angelo, Waco, Temple, Alexandria, Natchez, Hattiesburg, Dothan, Mobile, Pensacola

Pta. Sta. Eugenia, S. Quintin, San Jorge B., Agua Prieta, Cananea, Nacozari, Galeana, Villa Ahumada, Madera, Rio Grande, Brownwood, Austin, Houston, Beaumont, Lake Charles, Lafayette, Baton Rouge, New Orleans, C. San Blas

Hermosillo, Tiburón, Sonora, Ures, Torres, Empalme, Guaymas, Chihuahua, Conchos, San Antonio, Port Arthur B., Galveston, Atchafalaya B., Mississippi Delta

B. Ballenas, Sta. Rosalía, Muleje, Ciudad Obregón, Navojoa, Huatabampo, El Fuerte, Los Mochis, Jimenez, Hidalgo del Parral, Ciudad Camargo, Delicias, Piedras Negras, Nueva Rosita, Sabinas, Eagle Pass, Laredo, Nuevo Laredo, Corpus Christi, Padre I., Matagorda I.

La Purísima, B. La Paz, Sinaloa, Guamúchil, Culiacán, Elota, S. Pedro, Torreón, Lerdo, Gómez Palacio, Saltillo, Monclova, Falcon Res., Sabinas Hidalgo, Reynosa, Matamoros, Brownsville, Rio Grande del Norte, GULF OF MEXICO

C. San Lucas, Mazatlán, Rosario, Durango, Sombrerete, Concepcion del Oro, Matehuala, Monterrey, Montemorelos, S. Fernando, Laguna Madre

PACIFIC OCEAN, C. San Lucas, Escuinapa, Acaponeta, Fresnillo, Zacatecas, Charcas, Ciudad Victoria, Tula, Ciudad Mante, Tropic of Cancer

Is. Tres Marías, Tuxpan, Tepic, San Luis Potosí, Panuco, Ciudad Madero, Tampico, C. Rojo

C. Corrientes, Guadalajara, Ameca, Zacoalco, L. de Chapala, Santiago, León, Aguascalientes, Guanajuato, Irapuato, Celaya, Querétaro, Pachuca, Papantla, Tuxpan

Manzanillo, Colima Vol., Colima, Morelia, MEXICO, Toluca, Cuernavaca, Iguala, Tlaxcala, Puebla, Jalapa Enriquez, Veracruz, Golfo de Campeche, Mérida, Valladolid, I. de Cozumel, Peto, Vigia Chico

Balsas, Chilpancingo, Chilapa, Ayutla, Oaxaca, Orizaba, Tlacotalpan, Alvarado, Ciudad del Carmen, Coatzacoalcos, Laguna de Terminos, Carrillo Puerto, Yucatan, Ciudad Chetumal

Acapulco, Ometepec, Istmo de Tehuantepec, Juchitan, Chiapa, Tuxtla Gutierrez, Villahermosa, Usumacinta, Coroza, Ambergris Cay, Belize, Belmopan, BELIZE, Turneffe Is.

G. de Tehuantepec, Salina Cruz, Tonala, San Cristóbal, GUATEMALA, Guatemala, Middlesex, Golfo de Honduras, Pto. Barrios, Pto. Cortés, Telaa, Trujillo

Tehuantepec, G. de Huixtla, Sta. Ana, San José, San Salvador, EL SALVADOR, San Miguel, La Ceiba, Zacapa, Pedro Sula, HONDURAS, Comayagua, Tegucigalpa

Sonsonate, San Vicente, Choluteca, G. de Fonseca, Amapala, León, Managua, Masaya, NICARAGUA, Chinandega, Pen. de Nicoya, Puntarenas

PANAMA CANAL
1 : 1 000 000

14, Colón, Fort Randolph, Coco Solo, Cativa, Pta. Toro, Sherman, France Field, Cristobal, Silver City, Margarita, Fort Gulick, Fort Davis, Gatun, Gatun Locks, Gatun Dam, Las Deliciás, El Limon, Zorra, Monte Lirio, I. Madden, Madden Dam, I. Juan Gallegos, Escobal, Frijoles, Colorado, Darien, Chagres, Gamboa, South, Los Cascadas, Summit, Balboa Hill, Paraíso, Pedro Miguel, Red Tank, Culebra, R. Grande, Pedro Miguel Locks, Fort Clayton, Corozal, Curundu, Miraflores Locks, Diablo Heights, Fort Amador, Arraiján, La Boca, Howard Field, Balboa, Golfo, Panama, La Chorrera, PANAMA

JAMAICA
1 : 5 000 000

15, 16, 17, Lucea, Montego Bay, Falmouth, St. Ann's Bay, Galina Point, Cambridge, Newmarket, Frankfield, Albany, Port Maria, Annotto Bay, Port Antonio, Savanna la Mar, Black River, Ewarton, Spanish Town, KINGSTON, Port Royal, Port Morant, Morant Point, May Pen, Portland Point

TRINIDAD AND TOBAGO
1 : 5 000 000

19, 20, 21, Charlotteville, Moriah, Tobago, Canaan, Scarborough, Port of Spain, Blanchisseuse, Arima, Tunapuna, Songre Grande, Golfo de Paria, San Fernando, Rio Claro, Princes Town, TRINIDAD, Point Fortin, Siparia, Erin, Palo Seco, Boca de la Sierpe, Projection: Bonne

LEEWARD ISLANDS
1 : 5 000 000

18, 19, 20, 21, Anguilla (Br.), St. Martin (Fr.), Marigot, St. Maarten (Neth.), St. Barthélemy (Fr.), Saba (Neth.), St. Eustatius (Neth.), Codrington, Barbuda, ANTIGUA & BARBUDA, ST. CHRISTOPHER-NEVIS, Basseterre, Charlestown, St. John's, Antigua, Redonda, Montserrat, Plymouth, GUADELOUPE (Fr.), Guadeloupe Passage, Grande Terre, Le Moule, Désirade (Fr.), Ste. Rose, Ste. Anne, Basse Terre, Pointe-à-Pitre, Capesterre, Marie-Galante, I. des Saintes (Fr.), Grand Bourg, Dominica Passage, Portsmouth, Petit Marigot, Morne Diablotin, DOMINICA, Roseau, Scotts Head, Windward Is.

WINDWARD ISLANDS
1 : 5 000 000

20, 21, 22, Martinique Passage, Mt. Pelée 1463, Ste. Marie, Trinité, St. Pierre, Le Robert, Fort de France, Lamentin, Le Francois, Riviere Pilote, MARTINIQUE (Fr.), Ste. Anne, St. Lucia Channel, Castries, Soufrière, ST. LUCIA, Vieux Fort, St. Vincent Passage, Soufrière 1234, Georgetown, ST. VINCENT, Kingstown, BARBADOS, Speightstown, Bridgetown, Crane, Bequia, Port Elizabeth, THE GRENADINES, Mustique, Canouan, Union, The Grenadines, Carriacou, Hillsborough, Mt. Ronde, St. Catherine 840, St. George's, GRENADA, Grenville, Pointe Saline

1:15 000 000

100   0   100   200   300   400 miles
100   0   100 200 300 400 500 600 km

8   **9**   **10**   **11**

A

B

ATLANTIC OCEAN

Bermuda
⊙ Hamilton

Columbia
Atlanta
⊙ Augusta
C. Fear
Long Bay
⊙ Macon
lumbus
Savannah
⊙ C. Royal
Charleston
Albany
Altamaha
llahassee

Jacksonville

Daytona Beach

Orlando ⊙
C. Canaveral

Tampa
rsburg
Lakeland
West Palm Beach
Sarasota
L. Okeechobee
Fort
Lauderdale
Grand
Bahama
I.
Freeport
Gt. Abaco I.
New Providence I.

Miami

C. Sable

Key West
Nassau ⊙
Cat I.
S. Salvador
or Watlings I.

Florida Str.
BAHAMAS
Andros I.
Eleuthera I.

Tropic of Cancer

La Habana
(Havana)
arianao ⊙
Matanzas
Cárdenas
Colón
Long I.
Mayaguana

Sagua la Grande
Sta. Clara
Caibarién
Acklins
I.
Caicos I. (Br.)

Rio
Guane
Batabanó
G. de
C
U
Morón
Camagüey
Holguin
Gt. Inagua
Turks Is.(Br.)

Cienfuegos
Trinidad
Sancti
Spiritus
Ciego de Avila
Nuevitas
B
Antilla
Martí
San Francisco de Macoris

I. de Juventud
Jucaro
A
Baracoa
Monte Cristi
Port de Paix
PUERTO RICO (U.S.A.)

G
R
Manzanillo
Guantánamo
Cap Haitien
Valverde
Pto. Plata
Santiago
St. Thomas (U.S.A.)
San Juan
Charlotte Amalie
Anguilla

Campechuela
2000
Santiago
de Cuba
Baracoa
S. Francisco de Macoris
Agadilla
Arecibo
Vieques
Virgin Is. (Br.)
Sombrero (Br.)
St. Martin (Fr. & Neth.)

Grand Cayman
(Br.)
E
A
Gonaives
St. Marc
La Vega
DOMINICAN
REP.
La Romana
Mayagüez
1338
Ponce
St. Croix
(U.S.A.)
ST. CHRISTOPHER -
NEVIS
ANTIGUA &

Montego Bay
R
St. Ann's Bay
Jérémie
Leogane
Azua
Bani
Guayama
Caguas
Christiansted
Basseterre
Nevis
BARBUDA
St. John's

Savanna la Mar
Kingston
P. Antonio
Port au Prince
Duverge
Barahona
S. Pedro de Macoris
Santo Domingo
Charlestown
Plymouth
Montserrat

JAMAICA
Spanish Town
Les Cayes
Jacmel
Hispaniola
Guadeloupe (Fr.)
Pointe à Pitre

TILLES
Marie Galante (Fr.)

Leeward
Islands
DOMINICA
Roseau

LESSER
Martinique (Fr.)

C. Gracias á Dios
L. Caratasca
Puerto Cabezas
CARIBBEAN SEA
Fort de France
Castries
ST. LUCIA
BARBADOS

ANTILLES
Windward
ST. VINCENT
& Kingstown
Bridgetown

Providencia
(Col.)
San Andrés
(Col.)
Pta. Gallinas
THE GRENADINES
Islands
GRENADA
St. George's
The Grenadines

ragua
Bluefields
Santa Marta
Pen. de la
Guajira
Riohacha
Golfo de Venezuela
Aruba (Neth.)
Curacao (Neth.)
Willemstad
Bonaire (Neth.)
La Blanquilla
(Ven.)

uan
Barranquilla
Soledad
Sierra Nevada
de Santa Marta
Coro
NETH.
ANTILLES
Pto. Cabello
Maiquetía
La Tortuga
(Ven.)
Margarita
La Asunción
Carúpano
TRINIDAD & TOBAGO
Port of Spain

Cartagena
Calamar
Plato
L. de
Maracaibo
Dabajuro
⊙ **Maracaibo**
Cabimas
Caracas
2596
Barcelona
Cumaná
G. de
Paria
San Fernando

Vol. Irazú
Limón
Colón
Sincere
Mompos
El Banco
Trujillo
Valera
Valencia
2580
Las Mercedes
Maturín
Delta of the
Orinoco
Georgetown

Vol. Chiriqui
3374
Panama
G. del
Darién
Corozal
Ocaña
Maracay
San Felipe
Barquisimeto
El Tigre
Tucupita
Ciudad
Guayana

Chitré
La
Palma
Turbo
Atrato
Cúcuta
Portuguesa
Calabozo
San Fernando
de Apure
Ciudad Bolívar
Tumeremo

Arch. de
las Perlas
El Real
Antioquia
Cauca
6007
Cord. de Mérida
Apure
Orinoco
El Callao

Coiba
Pen. de
Azuero
G. de
Panama
Quibdó
Pto.
Wilches
Pamplona
Rubia
San Cristóbal
Arauca
Arauca
Caicara
2285
Roraima
2810

G. de Cupica
Medellín
Berrio
Bucaramanga
Pto. Páez
Pto. Carreño
Caura
SURINAM

Pta. Charambirá
Manizales
Pereira
La Dorada
Tunja
Meta
Pto. Ayacucho
Sierra Pacaraima
1280

Cartago
Ibagué
Honda
Bogotá
Zipaquirá
COLOMBIA
VENEZUELA
GUYANA

Buenayentura
Buga
Armenia
Girardot
Sa. Parima

Palmira
Ibagué
5216
Cali
750
Neiva
Guaviare

Popayán
4646
Guaviare
Casiquiare
BRAZIL

West from Greenwich

80   **9**   **10**   **11**   **12**   **13**

COPYRIGHT. GEORGE PHILIP & SON. LTD.

30

25

20

15

10

1   2   3   4   5   6   7

NICARAGUA
Masaya
Granada Rama
Managua Juigalpa
Rivas L. de Nicaragua Bluefields
S. Juan del Sur San Juan San Juan del Norte
Islas del Maíz (Nic., U.S.)
I. de San Andrés (Colombia)
Cayos de Albuquerque (Colombia)

Pta. Gallinas
Pen. de la Guajira
Aruba (Neth.) Curaçao (Neth.) Willemstad Bonaire (Neth.)
I. de Aves (Ven.)
I. Los Roques (Ven.) I. Orchila (Ven.)
I. Blanquilla (Ven.)
Los Hermanos I. Margarita (Ven.)
St. George's **GRENADA**
The Grenadines
Tobago Scarborough
Port of Spain **TRINIDAD & TOBAGO**

Nicoya
Liberia
Puntarenas **COSTA RICA**
C. Blanco San José Cartago 3837
G. de Nicoya Turrialba
Bocas del Toro Almirante 3374 Volcán Barú
B. de Coronado David **PANAMÁ**
G. Dulce Pto. Armuelles La Chorrera
Golfo de Chiriquí Chitré Penonomé
Isla Coiba Pta. Mala Pen. de Azuero

Santa Marta Ciénaga
Riohacha Uribía
Barranquilla Sabanalarga Soledad
Valledupar
Cartagena Turbaco Calamar Fundación
Sincelejo Magangué El Banco
Montería Mompós
Golfo del Darién Caucasia Ayapel
Arch. de las Perlas El Real Jurado
G. de Urabá Turbo Ríosucio
Quibdó
Istmina
C. Corrientes Andagoya
G. de Cupica

COLOMBIA
Medellín Rionegro
Manizales Pereira Cartago Armenia
Buenaventura **Cali** Palmira
Pta. Charambirá Tuluá
Popayán Huila 5750 Neiva
Pasto Mocoa
Tumaco Ipiales

Maracaibo Cabimas
Coro Punto Fijo La Vela
G. de Venezuela Altagracia de Orituco
Puerto Cabello **CARACAS**
Trujillo Barquisimeto **Valencia** Maracay
Lago de Maracaibo San Felipe San Juan de los Morros
La Ceiba Mérida Acarigua Calabozo
San Cristóbal Barinas San Fernando de Apure
Cúcuta Pamplona Guasdualito Arauca
VENEZUELA
Cumaná Carúpano
Barcelona La Cruz Maturín
El Tigre Tucupita
Ciudad Bolívar Ciudad Guayana (Santo Tomé) Upata
Orinoco Caicara
El Dorado Tumeremo
Sierra Pacaraima Mt. Roraima 2810

GUYANA
Georgetown Parika
Bartica Linden
RORAIMA
Boa Vista
Serra Acaraí

Bogotá Fusagasugá Villavicencio
Tunja Chiquinquirá Pto. Carreño
Bucaramanga Socorro San José del Guaviare
Barrancabermeja Guaviare
Orinoco Pto. Ayacucho
San Fernando de Atabapo
Pto. Leguízamo Mitú
Quito Cotopaxi 5896 Latacunga
Ambato Nuevo Rocafuerte
Chimborazo 6267 Riobamba
ECUADOR Sangay
Bahía de Caráquez Manta Portoviejo Babahoyo
Guayaquil Milagro Alausí 5230
Salinas Santa Elena Cuenca Azogues
G. de Guayaquil Machala Loja
Zorritos Tumbes

Negro
Barcelos
Carvoeiro Moura
Manaus
Manacapuru
AMAZONAS
Solimões (Amazonas)
Tefé Coari
São Paulo de Olivença
Benjamín Constant
Jutaí Juruá
Eirunepé
Tarauacá Feijó
Cruzeiro do Sul
ACRE Sena Madureira
Rio Branco Brasiléia
Xapuri Cobija
Porto Velho
RONDÔNIA
Guajará-Mirim Presidente Hermes
Riberalta
Villa Bella Sta. Rosa
BOLIVIA
Trinidad
L. Rogoaguado
Santa Ana L. Rogagua
Reyes Rurrenabaque San Borja
La Paz Cochabamba Santa Cruz
Illimani 6462 Oruro
Lago Titicaca 3812 Puno Sucre Potosí
Arequipa Moquegua Uyuni
Tacna Arica Iquique

PERU
Iquitos Requena
Contamana Pucallpa
Yurimaguas Moyobamba
Chachapoyas Tarapoto
Cajamarca Chiclayo Chimbote
Trujillo Salaverry Huaraz Huascarán 6768
Huánuco Cerro de Pasco
LIMA Callao Huancayo Ayacucho
Pisco Ica Cuzco
Huancavelica Abancay
Juliaca Puno Lago Titicaca
Arequipa Mollendo

PACIFIC OCEAN
Malpelo (Colombia)
I. Gorgona (Colombia)
Equator
Milne Edwards Trench
Peru-Chile Trench

ARGENTINA   **PARAGUAY**

1:16 000 000

100   0   100   200   300   400   500 miles
100   0   100 200 300 400 500 600 700 800 km

A T L A N T I C   O C E A N

Equator

SURINAM
FR. GUIANA
AMAPÁ
PARÁ
AMAZONAS
MARANHÃO
CEARÁ
RIO GRANDE DO NORTE
PARAIBA
PERNAMBUCO
ALAGOAS
SERGIPE
PIAUÍ
TOCANTINS
BAHIA
GOIÁS
MATO GROSSO
MATO GROSSO DO SUL
DIST. FED.
MINAS GERAIS
ESPIRITO SANTO
RIO DE JANEIRO
SÃO PAULO

B R A Z I L

Belém (Pará)
São Luís (Maranhão)
Teresina
Fortaleza (Ceará)
Natal
João Pessoa (Paraiba)
RECIFE (Pernambuco)
Olinda
Maceió
Aracaju
Salvador (Bahia)
Brasília
Goiânia
Belo Horizonte
Vitória
Niterói
RIO DE JANEIRO
SÃO PAULO
Campinas

Fernando de Noronha (Braz.)
Rocas
Trindade (Braz.)

Paramaribo
Nickerie
Nieuw Amsterdam
Cayenne
C. Orange
Oiapoque
C. do Norte
Ilha de Maracá
Macapá
Ilha de Marajó
Santarém
Óbidos
Monte Alegre
Altamira
Imperatriz
Sobral
Campina Grande
Caruaru
Penedo
Feira de Santana
Alagoinhas
Vitória da Conquista
Itabuna
Ilhéus
Montes Claros
Diamantina
Teófilo Otoni
Gov. Valadares
Juiz de Fora
Petrópolis
Campo Grande
Uberaba
Uberlândia

6059

COPYRIGHT. GEORGE PHILIP & SON, LTD.

Greenwich

1:16 000 000

100 50 0 100 200 300 miles
100 0 100 200 300 400 km

Countries and major regions

PARAGUAY
MATO GROSSO DO SUL
PARANÁ
SANTA CATARINA
RIO GRANDE DO SUL
URUGUAY
Chaco Boreal
Chaco Central

SOUTH ATLANTIC OCEAN

Peru-Chile Trench

Tropic of Capricorn

Cities and places

Rio de Janeiro
São Paulo
Santos
Curitiba
Paranaguá
Ponta Grossa
Pôrto Alegre
Pelotas
Rio Grande
Florianópolis
Blumenau
Caxias do Sul
Passo Fundo
Santa Maria
Asunción
Concepción
Villarrica
Encarnación
Posadas
Corrientes
Resistencia
Formosa
Tartagal
Orán
Salta
San Salvador de Jujuy
Antofagasta
Tocopilla
Copiapó
Chañaral
Caldera
La Serena
Coquimbo
Ovalle
San Miguel de Tucumán
Catamarca
Santiago del Estero
La Rioja
San Juan
Córdoba
Santa Fe
Paraná
Rosario
Mendoza
San Luis
Río Cuarto
Villa María
Viña del Mar
Valparaíso
Santiago
San Antonio
Rancagua
San Fernando
Curicó
Talca
Linares
Concepción
Talcahuano
Chillán
Los Angeles
Victoria
Temuco
Valdivia
Osorno
Puerto Montt
I. de Chiloé
Neuquén
Bahía Blanca
Buenos Aires
Avellaneda
La Plata
Montevideo
Mar del Plata
Necochea
Tandil
Azul
Olavarría
Santa Rosa
Viedma
San Antonio Oeste
Carmen de Patagones
Trelew
Rawson
Comodoro Rivadavia
Puerto Madryn
Península Valdés
Golfo Nuevo
Golfo San Jorge
Golfo San Matías
San Julián
Santa Cruz
Río Gallegos
Punta Arenas
Porvenir
Tierra del Fuego
I. de los Estados (Staten I.)
Cabo de Hornos (C. Horn)
Beagle Canal
Estrecho de Magallanes (Magellan's Str.)
Archipiélago de los Chonos
I. Wellington
Pen. de Taitao
G. de Penas
Canal Concepción

FALKLAND ISLANDS (ISLAS MALVINAS) (Br.)
West Falkland
East Falkland
Stanley
Jason Is
Weddell I.

South Georgia (Br.)

Rivera
Tacuarembó
Durazno
Treinta y Tres
Mercedes
Florida
Minas
Rocha
Maldonado

5830

Projection: Sanson-Flamsteed's Sinusoidal

West from Greenwich

COPYRIGHT GEORGE PHILIP & SON, LTD.

INDEX

The index contains the names of all the principal places and features shown on the maps. Each name is followed by an additional entry in italics giving the country or region within which it is located.

Physical features composed of a proper name (Erie) and a description (Lake) are positioned alphabetically by the proper name. The description is positioned after the proper name and is usually abbreviated.

The number in bold type which follows each name in the index refers to the number of the map page where that feature or place will be found. This is usually the largest scale at which the place or feature appears. The letter and figure which are in bold type immediately after the page number give the grid square on the map page, within which the feature is situated. The letter represents the latitude and the figure the longitude.

In some cases the feature itself may fall within the specified square, while the name is outside. This is usually the case only with features which are larger than a grid square. Rivers are indexed to their mouths or confluences, and carry the symbol ≈ after their names. A solid square ■ follows the name of a country while, an open square □ refers to a first order administrative area.

Abbreviations used in the index:

Afghan - Afghanistan	Dom. Rep. - Dominican Republic	Mt(s). - Mount(s), Mountains(s)	S. - South
Arch. - Archipelago	Eq. - Equatorial	N. - North	S. Arabia - Saudi Arabia
Amer. - America	Fin. - Finland	N.Z. - New Zealand	Str. - Strait
Atl. - Atlantic	G. - Gulf	Neth. - Netherlands	Swed. - Sweden
B. - Bay	Ger. - Germany	Norw. - Norway	Switz. - Switzerland
Bulg. - Bulgaria	I(s). - Island(s), Isle(s)	Pac. - Pakistan	U.A.E. - United Arab Emirates
C. - Cape	Ind. - Indian	Pen. - Peninsula	U.K. - United Kingdom
Cent. - Central	Ire. - Ireland	Port. - Portugal	U.S.A. - United States of America
Chan. - Channel	L. - Lake, Loch, Lough	Rep. - Republic	W. - West
Den. - Denmark	Mong. - Mongolia	Rom. - Romania	Yug. - Yugoslavia

A

Aachen, *Ger.* 16 C3
Aba, *Nigeria* 26 G6
Abadan, *Iran* 25 B3
Abashiri, *Japan* 21 F11
Abbeville, *France* 12 A4
Abeokuta, *Nigeria* 26 G5
Aberdare, *U.K.* 9 F4
Aberdeen, *U.K.* 10 D6
Aberystwyth, *U.K.* 9 E3
Abidjan, *Ivory Coast* 26 G4
Abilene, *U.S.A.* 36 D7
Abruzzi, □ *Italy* 14 C5
Abu Dhabi, *U.A.E.* 25 C4
Acapulco, *Mexico* 38 D5
Accra, *Ghana* 26 G4
Achill I., *Ire.* 11 C1
Aconcagua, *Argentina* 42 C3
Acre, □ *Brazil* 40 E4
Adamaoua, Massif de l', *Cameroon* 28 C2
Adana, *Turkey* 25 B2
Addis Abeba, *Ethiopia* 28 C7
Adelaide, *Australia* 33 E6
Aden, Gulf of, *Asia* 25 D3
Adriatic Sea, *Italy* 14 C6
Ægean Sea, *Greece* 15 E11
Afghanistan, ■ *Asia* 25 B5
Africa 30
Agadir, *Morocco* 26 B3
Agra, *India* 24 C4
Aguascalientes, *Mexico* 38 C4
Ahaggar, *Algeria* 26 D6
Ahmadabad, *India* 24 D3
Ahvaz, *Iran* 25 B3
Airdrie, *U.K.* 10 F5
Ajaccio, *France* 14 D3
Akershus, *Norw.* 7 F11
Akita, *Japan* 21 G11
Akron, *U.S.A.* 37 B10
Akureyri, *Iceland* 6 D4
Al 'Adan, *Yemen* 25 D3
Al Basrah, *Iraq* 25 B3
Al Hillah, *Iraq* 25 B3
Al Hufûf, *S. Arabia* 25 C3
Al Kut, *Iraq* 25 B3
Al Kuwayt, *Kuwait* 25 C3
Al Madinah, *S. Arabia* 25 C2
Al Manamãh, *S. Arabia* 25 C4
Al Mawsil, *Iraq* 25 B3
Al Qatif, *S. Arabia* 25 C3
Alabama, □ *U.S.A.* 37 D9
Alagôas, □ *Brazil* 41 E11
Alagoinhas, *Brazil* 41 F11
Aland, *Fin.* 7 F16
Alaska, □ *U.S.A.* 34 B4
Alba Iulia, *Rom.* 17 E11
Albacete, *Spain* 13 C5
Albania, ■ *Europe* 15 D9
Albany, *U.S.A.* 37 B12
Alberta, □ *Canada* 34 C8
Ålborg, *Den.* 7 H10
Albuquerque, *U.S.A.* 36 C5
Aldabra Is., *Africa* 30 F8
Alderney, *Channel Is.* 12 B2
Aldershot, *U.K.* 9 F7
Aleppo = Halab, *Syria* 25 B2
Alessándria, *Italy* 14 B3
Alesund, *Norw.* 6 F9
Aleutian Is., *U.S.A.* 34 C2
Alexandria = El Iskandarîya, *Egypt* 27 B10
Alfreton, *U.K.* 8 D6
Algarve, □ *Port.* 13 D1

Alger, *Algeria* 26 A5
Algeria, ■ *Africa* 26 C5
Algiers = Alger, *Algeria* 26 A5
Alicante, *Spain* 13 C5
Alice Springs, *Australia* 32 C5
Alkmaar, *Neth.* 16 B2
Allahabad, *India* 24 C5
Allentown, *U.S.A.* 37 B11
Alloa, *U.K.* 10 E5
Alma Ata, *Kazakhstan* 18 E8
Almeria, *Spain* 13 D4
Alps, *Europe* 12 D7
Alsace, □ *France* 12 B7
Altona, *Ger.* 16 B4
Ålvsborg, □ *Swed.* 7 G12
Amagasaki, *Japan* 21 B4
Amapá, □ *Brazil* 41 C8
Amarillo, *U.S.A.* 36 C6
Amazonas, ≈ *S. Amer.* 41 D8
Amazonas, □ *Brazil* 40 D5
Amiens, *France* 12 B5
Ammãn, *Jordan* 25 B2
Amritsar, *India* 24 B3
Amsterdam, *Neth.* 16 B2
Amundsen Gulf, *Canada* 34 A7
An Najaf, *Iraq* 25 B3
Anaheim, *U.S.A.* 36 D3
Anápolis, *Brazil* 41 G9
Anchorage, *Alaska* 34 B5
Ancohuma, *Bolivia* 40 G5
Ancona, *Italy* 14 C5
Andalucía, □ *Spain* 13 D3
Andaman Is., *India* 24 F7
Andes, Cord. de los, *S. Amer.* 40 G4
Andhra Pradesh, □ *India* 24 E4
Andorra, ■ *Europe* 13 A6
Andria, *Italy* 14 D7
Andros, *Greece* 15 F11
Andros I., *W. Indies* 39 C9
Angers, *France* 12 C3
Anglesey, *U.K.* 8 D3
Angola, ■ *Africa* 29 G3
Angoulême, *France* 12 D4
Angoumois, □ *France* 12 D3
Anguilla, *W. Indies* 38 J19
Anjou, □ *France* 12 C3
Ankara, *Turkey* 25 B2
Annaba, *Algeria* 26 A6
Anshan, *China* 22 B7
Antananarivo, *Madagascar* 29 H9
Antarctica 4 24C
Anticosti, Î. d', *Canada* 35 D13
Antigua & Barbuda, ■ *W. Indies* 38 K20
Antofagasta, *Chile* 42 A2
Antrim, *U.K.* 11 B5
Antwerpen, *Belgium* 16 C2
Aomori, *Japan* 21 F11
Apeldoorn, *Neth.* 16 B2
Appalachian Mts., *U.S.A.* 37 C10
Appennini, *Italy* 14 C5
Ar Ramadi, *Iraq* 25 B3
Ar Riyãd, *S. Arabia* 25 C3
Arabian Sea, *Asia* 25 D5
Aracajú, *Brazil* 41 F11
Arad, *Rom.* 17 E10
Aragón, □ *Spain* 13 B5
Arãk, *Iran* 25 B3
Aral Sea = Aralskoye More, *Asia* 18 E6
Aralskoye More, *Asia* 18 E6
Arbil, *Iraq* 25 B3
Arbroath, *U.K.* 10 E6
Arctic Ocean 4 12A
Ardabil, *Iran* 25 B3

Ardennes, *Belgium* 16 C2
Ardgour, *U.K.* 10 E3
Arenal, *Spain* 13 C7
Arequipa, *Peru* 40 G4
Argentina, ■ *S. Amer.* 42 E3
Århus, *Den.* 7 H11
Arizona, □ *U.S.A.* 36 D4
Arkansas, ≈ *U.S.A.* 37 C7
Arkansas, □ *U.S.A.* 37 D8
Arkhangelsk, *Russia* 18 C5
Arklow, *Ire.* 11 D5
Armagh, *U.K.* 11 B5
Armenia, ■ *Asia* 18 E5
Armenia, *Colombia* 40 C3
Arnhem, *Neth.* 16 C2
Arnhem Land, *Australia* 32 A5
Arran, *U.K.* 10 F3
Artois, □ *France* 12 A5
Aru Is., *Indonesia* 23 D5
Arunachal Pradesh, □ *India* 24 C7
Asahikawa, *Japan* 21 F11
Ascension, *Atl. Ocean* 30 F2
Ascoli Piceno, *Italy* 14 C5
Ashkhabad, *Turkmenistan* 18 F6
Asmera, *Ethiopia* 28 A7
Assam □ *India* 24 C7
Astrakhan, *Russia* 18 E5
Asturias, □ *Spain* 13 A3
Asunción, *Paraguay* 42 B5
Aswân, *Egypt* 27 D11
Asyût, *Egypt* 27 C11
Athabasca, L., *Canada* 34 C9
Athens = Athínai, *Greece* 15 F10
Athínai, *Greece* 15 F10
Atlanta, *U.S.A.* 37 D10
Atlantic Ocean 2
Auckland, *N.Z.* 31 G5
Augsburg, *Ger.* 16 D5
Augusta, *U.S.A.* 37 D10
Aust-Agder, □ *Norw.* 7 G9
Austin, *U.S.A.* 36 D7
Australia, ■ *Australasia* 32
Australian Alps, *Australia* 33 F8
Australian Capital Territory, □ *Australia* 33 F8
Austria, ■ *Europe* 16 E6
Auvergne, □ *France* 12 D5
Aviemore, *U.K.* 10 D5
Avignon, *France* 12 D6
Avila, *Spain* 13 B3
Avon, □ *U.K.* 9 F5
Ayers Rock, *Australia* 32 D5
Ayr, *U.K.* 10 F4
Azerbaijan, ■ *Asia* 18 E5
Azores, *Atl. Ocean* 2 C8
Azovskoye More, *Ukraine* 18 E4

B

Bãbol, *Iran* 25 B4
Bacãu, *Rom.* 17 E13
Bacabal, *Brazil* 41 D10
Badajoz, *Spain* 13 C2
Badalona, *Spain* 13 B7
Baden-Württemberg, □ *Ger.* 16 D4
Badenoch, *U.K.* 10 E4
Baffin Bay, *N. Amer.* 35 A13
Baffin I., *Canada* 35 B12
Baghdãd, *Iraq* 25 B3
Bahamas, ■ *W. Indies* 39 C10
Bahia, □ *Brazil* 41 F10

Bahía Blanca, *Argentina* 42 D4
Bahrain, ■ *Asia* 25 C4
Baidoa, *Somalia* 30 F8
Baja California, □ *Mexico* 38 B2
Bakersfield, *U.S.A.* 36 C3
Bakhtaran, *Iran* 25 B3
Baku, *Azerbaijan* 18 E5
Balboa, *Panama* 38 H14
Baleares, Is., *Spain* 13 C6
Bali, *Indonesia* 23 D3
Balkhash, Ozero, *Kazakhstan* 18 E8
Ballarat, *Australia* 33 F7
Ballater, *U.K.* 10 D5
Ballina, *U.K.* 11 B5
Ballymena, □ *U.K.* 11 B5
Ballymoney, □ *U.K.* 11 A5
Balmoral, *U.K.* 10 D5
Baltic Sea, *Europe* 7 H15
Baltimore, *U.S.A.* 37 C11
Bamako, *Mali* 26 F3
Bamberg, *Ger.* 16 D5
Bambridge, *U.K.* 11 B5
Bandon, *Ire.* 11 E3
Bandung, *Indonesia* 23 D2
Banff, *U.K.* 10 D6
Bangalore, *India* 24 F4
Banghâzi, *Libya* 27 B8
Bangkok, *Thailand* 23 B2
Bangladesh, ■ *Asia* 24 D6
Bangor, *U.K.* 11 B6
Bangui, *Cent. Afr. Rep.* 28 D3
Banjarmasin, *Indonesia* 23 D3
Banks I., *Canada* 34 A7
Bantry, *Ire.* 11 E2
Baotou, *China* 22 B5
Baranof I., *Alaska* 34 C6
Barbados, ■ *W. Indies* 38 P22
Barbuda, *W. Indies* 38 K20
Barcelona, *Spain* 13 B7
Bardsey I., *U.K.* 8 E3
Bareilly, *India* 24 C4
Barents Sea, *Arctic* 18 B4
Bari, *Italy* 14 D7
Barkly Tableland, *Australia* 32 B6
Barletta, *Italy* 14 D7
Barnsley, *U.K.* 8 D6
Barquisimeto, *Venezuela* 40 A5
Barra, *U.K.* 10 E1
Barrancabermeja, *Colombia* 40 B4
Barranquilla, *Colombia* 40 A4
Barrow-in-Furness, *U.K.* 8 C4
Barry, *U.K.* 9 F4
Basel, *Switz.* 16 E3
Basildon, *U.K.* 9 F8
Basilicata, □ *Italy* 14 D6
Basingstoke, *U.K.* 9 F6
Bass Strait, *Australia* 33 F8
Basse Terre, *Guadeloupe* 38 L20
Bath, *U.K.* 9 F5
Baton Rouge, *U.S.A.* 37 D8
Bauru, *Brazil* 41 H9
Bayern, □ *Ger.* 16 D5
Baykal, Ozero, *Russia* 19 D11
Bayonne, *France* 12 E3
Bayrût, *Lebanon* 25 B2
Beaujolais, *France* 12 C6
Beaumont, *U.S.A.* 37 D8
Bedford, *U.K.* 9 E7
Bedfordshire, □ *U.K.* 9 E7
Beijing, *China* 22 C6
Beira, *Mozambique* 29 H7
Belcher Is., *Canada* 35 C12
Belém, *Brazil* 41 D9
Belet Uen, *Somalia* 30 F8

Belfast, *U.K.* 11 B6
Belgium, ■ *Europe* 16 C2
Belgrade = Beograd, *Yug.* 15 B9
Belize, ■ *Cent. Amer.* 38 D7
Belmopan, *Belize* 38 D7
Belo Horizonte, *Brazil* 41 G10
Belorussia, ■ *Europe* 18 D3
Beloye More, *Russia* 18 C4
Ben Nevis, *U.K.* 10 E4
Benares = Varanasi, *India* 24 C5
Benbecula, *U.K.* 10 D1
Bengal, B. of, *Ind. Ocean* 24 E6
Bengbu, *China* 22 C6
Benguela, *Angola* 29 G2
Beni Suef, *Egypt* 27 C11
Benidorm, *Spain* 13 C5
Benin, ■ *Africa* 26 G5
Benin, Bight of, *Africa* 26 H5
Benin City, *Nigeria* 26 G6
Benoni, *S. Africa* 29 K5
Benue, ≈ *Africa* 26 G6
Benxi, *China* 22 B7
Beograd, *Yug.* 15 B9
Bergamo, *Italy* 14 B3
Bergen, *Norw.* 7 F8
Bering Sea, *Arctic* 19 D17
Berkeley, *U.S.A.* 36 C2
Berkshire, □ *U.K.* 9 F6
Berlin, *Ger.* 16 B6
Bermuda, □ *Atl. Ocean* 39 A12
Bern, *Switz.* 16 E3
Berwick-upon-Tweed, *U.K.* 8 B6
Besançon, *France* 12 C7
Béziers, *France* 12 E5
Bhopal, *India* 24 D4
Bhutan, ■ *Asia* 24 C7
Białystok, *Poland* 17 B11
Biarritz, *France* 12 E3
Biel, *Switz.* 16 E3
Bielefeld, *Ger.* 16 B4
Bielsko-Biała, *Poland* 17 D9
Bihar, □ *India* 24 D6
Bijagos, Arquipélago dos, *Guinea-Bissau* 26 F1
Bilbao, *Spain* 13 A4
Billings, *U.S.A.* 36 A5
Bioko, Eq. Guinea 28 D1
Birkenhead, *U.K.* 8 D4
Birmingham, *U.K.* 9 E6
Birmingham, *U.S.A.* 37 D9
Biscay, B. of, *Europe* 12 D1
Bishkek, *Kirghizia* 18 E8
Bishop Auckland, *U.K.* 8 C6
Bitola, *Macedonia* 15 D9
Biwa-Ko, *Japan* 21 B5
Black Sea, *Europe* 18 E4
Blackburn, *U.K.* 8 D5
Blackpool, *U.K.* 8 D4
Blanc, Mt., *France* 12 D7
Blantyre, *Malawi* 29 H7
Blaydon, *U.K.* 8 C6
Blekinge, □ *Swed.* 7 H13
Bloemfontein, *S. Africa* 29 K5
Blue Nile = Nîl el Azraq, ≈ *Africa* 27 E11
Blyth, *U.K.* 8 B6
Bobo-Dioulasso, *Burkina Faso* 26 F4
Bochum, *Ger.* 16 C3
Boden, *Swed.* 6 D16
Bodmin Moor, *U.K.* 9 G3
Boggeragh Mts., *Ire.* 11 D3
Bogotá, *Colombia* 40 C4
Böhmerwald, *Ger.* 16 D6
Bolivia, ■ *S. Amer.* 40 G5

Index

Bologna, *Italy* 14 B4
Bolton, *U.K.* 8 D5
Bombay, *India* 24 E4
Bonn, *Ger.* 16 C3
Boothia, Gulf of, *Canada* 35 A11
Bootle, *U.K.* 8 D4
Borås, *Swed.* 7 H12
Bordeaux, *France* 12 D3
Borders, □ *U.K.* 10 F5
Borlänge, *Swed.* 7 F13
Borneo, □ *Indonesia* 23 C3
Bornholm, *Den.* 7 J13
Bosnia-Herzegovina, ■ *Europe* 14 B7
Bosporus, *Turkey* 25 A1
Boston, *U.S.A.* 37 B12
Boston, *U.K.* 8 E7
Bothnia, G. of, *Scandinavia* 6 E16
Botoşani, *Rom.* 17 E13
Botswana, ■ *Africa* 29 J4
Bouaké, *Ivory Coast* 26 G3
Boulogne, *France* 12 A4
Bourbonnais, □ *France* 12 C5
Bourges, *France* 12 C5
Bournemouth, *U.K.* 9 G6
Bowland, Forest of, *U.K.* 8 D5
Boyne, ≈ *Ire.* 11 C5
Brăila, *Rom.* 17 F13
Bradford, *U.K.* 8 D6
Braga, *Port.* 13 B1
Brahmaputra, ≈ *India* 24 C7
Brandenburg, *Ger.* 16 B6
Brantford, *Canada* 35 D11
Brasília, *Brazil* 41 G9
Braşov, *Rom.* 17 F12
Bratislava, *Slovak Rep.* 16 D8
Bratsk, *Russia* 19 D11
Braunschweig, *Ger.* 16 B5
Bray, *Ire.* 11 C5
Brazil, ■ *S. Amer.* 41 F8
Brazzaville, *Congo* 28 E3
Breadalbane, *U.K.* 10 E4
Brecon Beacons, *U.K.* 9 F4
Breda, *Neth.* 16 C2
Bremen, *Ger.* 16 B4
Bremerhaven, *Ger.* 16 B4
Brentwood, *U.K.* 9 F8
Bréscia, *Italy* 14 B4
Bressay, *U.K.* 10 A7
Brest, *France* 12 B1
Bretagne, □ *France* 12 B2
Bridgeport, *U.S.A.* 37 B12
Bridgetown, *Barbados* 38 P22
Bridgwater, *U.K.* 9 F4
Bridlington, *U.K.* 8 C7
Brighton, *U.K.* 9 G7
Bríndisi, *Italy* 15 D7
Brisbane, *Australia* 33 D9
Bristol, *U.K.* 9 F5
Bristol Channel, *U.K.* 9 F3
British Columbia, □ *Canada* 34 C7
Brno, *Czech Rep.* 16 D8
Broads, The, *U.K.* 8 E9
Brooks Range, *Alaska* 34 B5
Brugge, *Belgium* 16 C1
Brunei, ■ *Asia* 23 C3
Brussel, *Belgium* 16 C2
Bruxelles = Brussel, *Belgium* 16 C2
Bucaramanga, *Colombia* 40 B4
Buchan, *U.K.* 10 D6
Bucharest = Bucureşti, *Rom.* 17 F13
Buckinghamshire, □ *U.K.* 9 F7
Bucureşti, *Rom.* 17 F13
Budapest, *Hungary* 17 E9
Buenaventura, *Colombia* 40 C3
Buenos Aires, *Argentina* 42 C5
Buffalo, *U.S.A.* 37 B11
Buga, *Colombia* 40 C3
Bujumbura, *Burundi* 28 E5
Bukavu, *Zaïre* 28 E5
Bulawayo, *Zimbabwe* 29 J5
Bulgaria, ■ *Europe* 15 C11
Bûr Saîd, *Egypt* 27 B11
Bûr Sûdân, *Sudan* 27 E12
Burgas, *Bulg.* 15 C12
Burgenland, □ *Austria* 16 E8
Burgos, *Spain* 13 A4
Burkina Faso, ■ *Africa* 26 F4
Burma, ■ *Asia* 24 D8
Bursa, *Turkey* 25 A1
Burton-on-Trent, *U.K.* 8 E6
Buru, *Indonesia* 23 D4
Burundi, ■ *Africa* 28 E5
Buskerud, □ *Norw.* 7 F10
Bute, *U.K.* 10 F3
Bydgoszcz, *Poland* 17 B8
Bylot I., *Canada* 35 A12
Bytom, *Poland* 17 C9

C

Cabimas, *Venezuela* 40 A4
Cabinda, □ *Angola* 28 F2
Cáceres, *Spain* 13 C2
Cádiz, *Spain* 13 D2
Caen, *France* 12 B3
Caernarfon B., *U.K.* 8 D3
Cágliari, *Italy* 14 E3
Caha Mts., *Ire.* 11 E2
Cairngorm Mts., *U.K.* 10 D5

Cairo = El Qâhira, *Egypt* 27 B11
Calabar, *Nigeria* 26 G6
Calabria, □ *Italy* 14 E7
Calais, *France* 12 A4
Calcutta, *India* 24 D6
Calgary, *Canada* 34 C8
Cali, *Colombia* 40 C3
Calicut, *India* 24 F4
California, □ *U.S.A.* 36 C2
Callao, *Peru* 40 F3
Caltanissetta, *Italy* 14 F5
Camagüey, *Cuba* 39 C9
Cambodia, ■ *Asia* 23 B7
Camborne, *U.K.* 9 G2
Cambrian Mts., *U.K.* 9 E4
Cambridge, *U.K.* 9 E8
Cambridgeshire, □ *U.K.* 9 E8
Camden, *U.S.A.* 37 C12
Cameroon, ■ *Africa* 28 C2
Cameroon, Mt., *Cameroon* 28 D1
Campania, □ *Italy* 14 D6
Campbeltown, *U.K.* 10 F3
Campeche, G. de, *Mexico* 38 D6
Campina Grande, *Brazil* 41 E12
Campinas, *Brazil* 41 H9
Campo Grande, *Brazil* 41 H8
Campos, *Brazil* 41 H10
Canada, ■ *N. Amer.* 34 C10
Canarias, Is., *Atl. Ocean* 26 C1
Canaveral, C., *U.S.A.* 37 E10
Canberra, *Australia* 33 F8
Cannes, *France* 12 E7
Canouan, *W. Indies* 38 Q20
Cantabria, □ *Spain* 13 A3
Canterbury, *U.K.* 9 F9
Canton = Guangzhou, *China* 22 D6
Cape Province, □ *S. Africa* 29 L4
Cape Town, *S. Africa* 29 L3
Cape York Pen., *Australia* 33 A7
Caprivi Strip, *Namibia* 29 H4
Caracas, *Venezuela* 40 A5
Caratinga, *Brazil* 41 G10
Cardiff, *U.K.* 9 F4
Cardigan B., *U.K.* 9 E3
Carlisle, *U.K.* 8 C5
Carlow, *Ire.* 11 D5
Carmarthen B., *U.K.* 9 F3
Carnegie, L., *Australia* 32 D3
Caroline Is., *Pac. Ocean* 3 D17
Carpathians, *Europe* 17 E12
Carpentaria, Gulf of, *Australia* 33 A6
Carrara, *Italy* 14 B4
Carrickfergus, *U.K.* 11 B6
Cartagena, *Spain* 13 D5
Cartagena, *Colombia* 40 A3
Cartago, *Colombia* 40 C3
Caruaru, *Brazil* 41 E11
Carúpano, *Venezuela* 40 A6
Casablanca, *Morocco* 26 B3
Caspian Sea, *Asia* 18 E6
Castellón de la Plana, *Spain* 13 C5
Castilla - La Mancha, □ *Spain* 13 C3
Castilla y Leon, □ *Spain* 13 B3
Castries, *St. Lucia* 38 N21
Cataluña, □ *Spain* 13 B6
Catánia, *Italy* 14 F6
Catanzaro, *Italy* 14 E7
Caviana, I., *Brazil* 41 C9
Cavan, □ *Ire.* 11 B4
Cebu, *Philippines* 23 B4
Cedar L., *Canada* 34 C10
Celebes Sea, *Asia* 23 C4
Celebes = Sulawesi, *Indonesia* 23 D4
Ceram, *Indonesia* 23 D4
Cerignola, *Italy* 14 D6
Ceylon = Sri Lanka, ■ *Asia* 24 G5
Chad, ■ *Africa* 27 E8
Champagne, □ *France* 12 B6
Chang, ≈ *China* 22 C7
Changchun, *China* 22 B7
Changsha, *China* 22 D6
Changzhou, *China* 22 C7
Channel Is., *U.K.* 12 B2
Charleston, *U.S.A.* 37 D10
Charlotte, *U.S.A.* 37 C10
Charlottenburg, *Ger.* 16 B6
Charlottetown, *Canada* 35 D13
Chatham, *U.K.* 9 F8
Chattanooga, *U.S.A.* 37 C9
Cheju Do, *S. Korea* 22 C7
Chelmsford, *U.K.* 9 F8
Cheltenham, *U.K.* 9 F5
Chelyabinsk, *Russia* 18 D7
Chemnitz, *Ger.* 16 C6
Chengdu, *China* 22 C5
Cherbourg, *France* 12 B3
Cheremkhovo, *Russia* 19 D11
Chesapeake B., *U.S.A.* 37 C11
Cheshire, □ *U.K.* 8 D5
Chester, *U.K.* 8 D5
Chesterfield, *U.K.* 8 D6
Cheviot Hills, *U.K.* 8 B5
Chiba, *Japan* 21 B7
Chicago, *U.S.A.* 37 B9
Chichagof I., *Alaska* 34 C6

Chiclayo, *Peru* 40 E3
Chihuahua, *Mexico* 38 B3
Chile, ■ *S. Amer.* 42 D2
Chiloe I. de, *Chile* 42 E2
Chiltern Hills, *U.K.* 9 F7
Chimborazo, *Ecuador* 40 D3
China, ■ *Asia* 22 C4
Chingola, *Zambia* 29 G5
Chişinau = Kishinev, *Moldavia* 18 E3
Chita, *Russia* 19 D12
Chittagong, *Bangladesh* 24 D7
Chongqing, *China* 22 D5
Chonos, Arch. de los, *Chile* 42 E2
Chorzów, *Poland* 17 C9
Christchurch, *N.Z.* 31 K4
Christmas I., *Australia* 23 E2
Chukotskoye More, *Russia* 19 C19
Chungking = Chongqing, *China* 22 D5
Ciénaga, *Colombia* 40 A4
Cienfuegos, *Cuba* 39 C8
Cincinnati, *U.S.A.* 37 C10
Ciudad Bolivar, *Venezuela* 40 B6
Ciudad Guayana, *Venezuela* 40 B6
Ciudad Juárez, *Mexico* 38 A3
Ciudad Real, *Spain* 13 C4
Clacton, *U.K.* 9 F9
Clare, □ *Ire.* 11 D2
Cleethorpes, *U.K.* 8 D7
Clermont-Ferrand, *France* 12 D5
Cleveland, *U.S.A.* 37 B10
Cleveland, □ *U.K.* 8 C6
Clonmel, *Ire.* 11 D4
Cluj-Napoca, *Rom.* 17 E11
Clwyd, □ *U.K.* 8 D4
Clyde, ≈ *U.K.* 10 F5
Clyde, Firth of, *U.K.* 10 F3
Clydebank, *U.K.* 10 F4
Coalville, *U.K.* 8 E6
Coast Ranges, *U.S.A.* 36 C2
Coatbridge, *U.K.* 10 F4
Coats I., *Canada* 35 B11
Cobh, *Ire.* 11 E3
Cochabamba, *Bolivia* 40 G5
Cocos or Keeling Is., *Australia* 23 E1
Coimbra, *Port.* 13 B1
Colchester, *U.K.* 9 F8
Coleraine, □ *U.K.* 11 A5
Coll, *U.K.* 10 E2
Cologne = Köln, *Ger.* 16 C3
Colombia, ■ *S. Amer.* 40 C4
Colombo, *Sri Lanka* 24 G5
Colón, *Panama* 39 H14
Colonsay, *U.K.* 10 E2
Colorado, □ *U.S.A.* 36 C5
Colorado, ≈ *U.S.A.* 36 D4
Colorado Springs, *U.S.A.* 36 C6
Columbia, ≈ *U.S.A.* 36 A2
Columbia, *U.S.A.* 37 D10
Columbus, Georgia, *U.S.A.* 37 D10
Columbus, Ohio, *U.S.A.* 37 C10
Colwyn Bay, *U.K.* 8 D4
Comeragh Mts., *Ire.* 11 D4
Como, *Italy* 14 B3
Comoros, ■ *Africa* 30 G8
Conakry, *Guinea* 26 G2
Concepcion, *Chile* 42 D2
Congo, ■ *Africa* 28 E3
Congo = Zaïre, ≈ *Africa* 28 D4
Connacht, *Ire.* 11 C2
Connecticut, □ *U.S.A.* 37 B12
Connemara, *Ire.* 11 C2
Constanţa, *Rom.* 17 F14
Constantine, *Algeria* 26 A6
Cookstown, *U.K.* 11 B5
Cooper Creek, ≈ *Australia* 33 D6
Copenhagen = København, *Den.* 7 J12
Córdoba, *Spain* 13 D3
Córdoba, *Argentina* 42 C4
Corfu = Kérkira, *Greece* 15 E8
Cork, *Ire.* 11 E3
Cornwall, □ *U.K.* 9 G3
Coronation Gulf, *Canada* 34 B8
Corpus Christi, *U.S.A.* 36 E7
Corse, *France* 14 C3
Corsica = Corse, *France* 14 C3
Corumba, *Brazil* 40 G7
Cosenza, *Italy* 14 E7
Costa Blanca, *Spain* 13 C5
Costa Brava, *Spain* 13 B7
Costa del Sol, *Spain* 13 D4
Costa Dorada, *Spain* 13 B7
Costa Rica, ■ *Cent. Amer.* 39 F8
Cote d'Ivoire = Ivory Coast,
  ■ *Africa* 26 G3
Cotonou, *Benin* 26 G5
Cotopaxi, *Ecuador* 40 D3
Cotswold Hills, *U.K.* 9 F5
Cottbus, *Ger.* 16 C7
Coventry, *U.K.* 9 E6
Craiova, *Rom.* 17 F11
Crawley, *U.K.* 9 F7
Cremona, *Italy* 14 B4
Crete = Kriti, *Greece* 15 G11
Crewe, *U.K.* 8 D5
Croatia, ■ *Europe* 14 B6
Cromarty, *U.K.* 10 D4
Cuba, ■ *W. Indies* 39 C8
Cúcuta, *Colombia* 40 B4
Cuenca, *Ecuador* 40 D3

Cuenca, *Spain* 13 B4
Cuiaba, *Brazil* 41 G7
Cumaná, *Venezuela* 40 A6
Cumbernauld, *U.K.* 10 F4
Cumbria, □ *U.K.* 8 C5
Cumbrian Mts., *U.K.* 8 C4
Curaçao, *Neth. Ant.* 40 A5
Curitiba, *Brazil* 42 B7
Cuzco, *Peru* 40 F4
Cwmbran, *U.K.* 9 F4
Cyclades = Kikládhes, *Greece* 15 F11
Cyprus, ■ *Asia* 25 B2
Czech Rep., ■ *Europe* 16 D7
Czestochowa, *Poland* 17 C9

D

Dakar, *Senegal* 26 F1
Dalian, *China* 22 C7
Dallas, *U.S.A.* 37 D7
Damaraland, *Namibia* 29 J3
Damascus = Dimashq, *Syria* 25 B2
Dandong, *China* 22 B7
Danube = Dunarea, ≈ *Europe* 17 F14
Dar-es-Salaam, *Tanzania* 28 F7
Dardanelles, *Turkey* 25 A1
Darién, G. del, *S. Amer.* 40 B3
Darling, ≈ *Australia* 33 E7
Darlington, *U.K.* 8 C6
Darmstadt, *Ger.* 16 D4
Dartmoor, *U.K.* 9 G4
Dartmouth, *Canada* 35 D13
Darwin, *Australia* 32 A5
Datong, *China* 22 B6
Dauphine, □ *France* 12 D6
Davao, *Philippines* 23 C4
Davis Str., *N. Amer.* 35 B14
Dayton, *U.S.A.* 37 C10
Dead Sea, *Asia* 25 B2
Deal, *U.K.* 9 F9
Dean, Forest of, *U.K.* 9 F5
Debrecen, *Hungary* 17 E10
Delaware, □ *U.S.A.* 37 C11
Delhi, *India* 24 C4
Denmark, ■ *Europe* 7 J10
Denver, *U.S.A.* 36 C6
Derby, *U.K.* 8 E6
Derbyshire, □ *U.K.* 8 D6
Derryveagh Mts., *Ire.* 11 A4
Des Moines, *U.S.A.* 37 B8
Dessau, *Ger.* 16 C6
Detroit, *U.S.A.* 37 B10
Devon, □ *U.K.* 9 G4
Devon I., *Canada* 35 A11
Dezfûl, *Iran* 25 B3
Dhaka, *Bangladesh* 24 D7
Dhodhekanisos, *Greece* 15 F12
Dieppe, *France* 12 B4
Dijon, *France* 12 C6
Dimashq, *Syria* 25 B2
Dingle B., *Ire.* 11 D1
Dingwall, *U.K.* 10 D4
Disappointment, L., *Australia* 32 C3
Diyarbakir, *Turkey* 25 B3
Djibouti, ■ *Africa* 30 D8
Dnepropetrovsk, *Ukraine* 18 E4
Dniestr, ≈ *Europe* 17 D11
Dolomiti, *Italy* 14 A4
Dominica, ■ *W. Indies* 38 M20
Dominican Rep., ■ *W. Indies* 39 D10
Don, ≈ *Russia* 18 E5
Doncaster, *U.K.* 8 D6
Donegal, *Ire.* 11 B3
Donetsk, *Ukraine* 18 E4
Dordrecht, *Neth.* 16 C2
Dornoch, *U.K.* 10 D4
Dorset, □ *U.K.* 9 G5
Dortmund, *Ger.* 16 C3
Douala, *Cameroon* 28 D1
Douglas, *U.K.* 8 C3
Dounreay, *U.K.* 10 C5
Douro, ≈ *Port.* 13 B1
Dover, *U.K.* 9 F9
Down, □ *U.K.* 11 B6
Drakensberg, *S. Africa* 29 K5
Drammen, *Norw.* 7 G11
Dresden, *Ger.* 16 C6
Drogheda, *Ire.* 11 C5
Dubai = Dubayy, *U.A.E.* 25 C4
Dublin, *Ire.* 11 C5
Dubrovnik, *Croatia* 15 C8
Dudley, *U.K.* 9 E5
Duisburg, *Ger.* 16 C3
Duluth, *U.S.A.* 37 A8
Dumbarton, *U.K.* 10 F4
Dumfries, *U.K.* 10 F5
Dumfries and Galloway, □ *U.K.* 10 F5
Dumyât, *Egypt* 27 B11
Dun Laoghaire, *Ire.* 11 C5
Dunarea, ≈ *Europe* 17 F14
Dundalk, *Ire.* 11 B5
Dundee, *U.K.* 10 E6
Dunedin, *N.Z.* 31 L3
Dunfermline, *U.K.* 10 E5
Dungannon, *U.K.* 11 B5
Dungarvan, *Ire.* 11 D4
Dunkerque, *France* 12 A5
Durango, *Mexico* 38 C4
Durban, *S. Africa* 29 K6
Durham, □ *U.K.* 8 C6
Dushanbe, *Tajikistan* 18 F7

Düsseldorf, *Ger.* 16 C3
Dyfed, □ *U.K.* 9 E3

E

East China Sea, *Asia* 22 D7
East Kilbride, *U.K.* 10 F4
East London, *S. Africa* 29 L5
East Siberian Sea, *Arctic* 19 B17
East Sussex, □ *U.K.* 9 G8
Eastbourne, *U.K.* 9 G8
Easter Is., *Pac. Ocean* 2 F4
Ebbw Vale, *U.K.* 9 F4
Ebro, ≈ *Spain* 13 B6
Ech Cheliff, *Algeria* 26 A5
Ecuador, ■ *S. Amer.* 40 D3
Eday, *U.K.* 10 B6
Edinburgh, *U.K.* 10 F5
Edmonton, *Canada* 34 C8
Edward, L., *Africa* 28 E5
Egypt, ■ *Africa* 27 D10
Eifel, *Ger.* 16 C3
Eigg, *U.K.* 10 E2
Eighty Mile Beach, *Australia* 32 B3
Eindhoven, *Neth.* 16 C2
El Faiyûm, *Egypt* 27 C11
El Ferrol, *Spain* 13 A1
El Gîza, *Egypt* 27 C11
El Iskandarîya, *Egypt* 27 B10
El Khartûm, *Sudan* 27 E11
El Mahalla el Kubra, *Egypt* 27 B11
El Mansûra, *Egypt* 27 B11
El Minyâ, *Egypt* 27 C11
El Obeid, *Sudan* 27 F11
El Paso, *U.S.A.* 36 D5
El Qâhira, *Egypt* 27 B11
El Salvador, ■ *Cent. Amer.* 38 E7
El Suweis, *Egypt* 27 C11
Elba, *Italy* 14 C4
Elbe, ≈ *Ger.* 16 B4
Elblag, *Poland* 17 A9
Elburz Mts., *Iran* 25 B4
Elche, *Spain* 13 C5
Eleuthera I., *W. Indies* 39 B9
Elgin, *U.K.* 10 D5
Ellesmere I., *Canada* 8 D5
Emilia Romagna, □ *Italy* 14 B4
England, □ *U.K.* 8 E6
English Channel, *Europe* 9 G6
Ennis, *Ire.* 11 D3
Enniscorthy, *Ire.* 11 D5
Enschede, *Neth.* 16 B3
Enugu, *Nigeria* 26 G6
Equatorial Guinea, ■ *Africa* 28 D1
Erawadi Myit, ≈ *Burma* 24 E8
Erfurt, *Ger.* 16 C5
Erie, L., *N. Amer.* 35 D11
Eritrea, □ *Ethiopia* 28 A7
Erzurum, *Turkey* 25 B3
Esbjerg, *Den.* 7 J10
Esfahân, *Iran* 25 B4
Eskilstuna, *Swed.* 7 G14
Eskisehir, *Turkey* 25 B2
Espirito Santo, □ *Brazil* 41 G10
Essen, *Ger.* 16 C3
Essex, □ *U.K.* 9 F8
Estonia, ■ *Europe* 18 D3
Ethiopia, ■ *Africa* 28 C7
Etna, Mt., *Italy* 14 F6
Euphrates, ≈ *Asia* 25 B3
Evansville, *U.S.A.* 37 C9
Everest, Mt., *Nepal* 24 C6
Everglades, *U.S.A.* 37 E10
Évora, *Port.* 13 C2
Évvoia, *Greece* 15 E11
Exeter, *U.K.* 9 G4
Exmoor, *U.K.* 9 F4
Extremadura, □ *Spain* 13 C2
Eyre, L., *Australia* 33 D6
Eyre Peninsula, *Australia* 32 E6

F

Fairbanks, *Alaska* 34 B5
Falkirk, *U.K.* 10 F5
Falkland Is, *Atl. Ocean* 42 G5
Fareham, *U.K.* 9 G6
Farnborough, *U.K.* 9 F7
Faroe Is., *Atl. Ocean* 5 C4
Feira de Santana, *Brazil* 41 F11
Fens, The, *U.K.* 8 E7
Fermanagh, □ *U.K.* 11 B4
Ferrara, *Italy* 14 B4
Fès, *Morocco* 26 B3
Fetlar, *U.K.* 10 A8
Fife, □ *U.K.* 10 E5
Fiji, ■ *Pac. Ocean* 31 C7
Finland, ■ *Europe* 6 C19
Finnmark, □ *Norw.* 6 B18
Firenze, *Italy* 14 C4
Flandre, *Belgium* 16 C1
Fleetwood, *U.K.* 8 D4
Flensburg, *Ger.* 16 A4
Flinders I., *Australia* 33 F8
Flint, *U.S.A.* 37 B10
Florence = Firenze, *Italy* 14 C4
Flores, *Indonesia* 23 D4
Florida, □ *U.S.A.* 37 E10
Fóggia, *Italy* 14 D6

olkestone, *U.K.* 9 F9
ort de France, *Martinique* 38 N20
ort Smith, *U.S.A.* 37 C8
ort Wayne, *U.S.A.* 37 B9
ort William, *U.K.* 10 E3
ort Worth, *U.S.A.* 36 D7
ortaleza, *Brazil* 41 D11
orth, Firth of, *U.K.* 10 E6
oula, *U.K.* 10 A6
oxe Channel, *Canada* 35 B11
rance, ■ *Europe* 12 C4
ranche-Comte, □ *France* 12 C6
rankfurt am Main, *Ger.* 16 C4
rankfurt an der Oder, *Ger.* 16 B7
ränkische Alb, *Ger.* 16 D5
raser I., *Australia* 33 D9
raserburgh, *U.K.* 10 D6
rederikshavn, *Den.* 7 H11
rederikstad, *Norw.* 7 G11
reetown, *Sierra Leone* 26 G2
reiburg, *Ger.* 16 D3
rench Guiana, ■ *S. Amer.* 41 C8
resno, *U.S.A.* 36 C3
riuli Venezia Giulia, □ *Italy* 14 A5
rome, L., *Australia* 33 E6
runze = Bishkek, *Kirghizia* 18 E8
uji-San, *Japan* 21 B6
ukuoka, *Japan* 21 C2
ukushima, *Japan* 21 G11
unabashi, *Japan* 21 B7
ürth, *Ger.* 16 D5
ushun, *China* 22 B7
uzhou, *China* 22 D6
yn, *Den.* 7 J11

G

Gabon, ■ *Africa* 28 E2
Gaborone, *Botswana* 29 J5
Gairdner, L., *Australia* 32 E6
Galaţi, *Rom.* 17 F14
Galapagos Is., *Pac. Ocean* 2 E5
Galashiels, *U.K.* 10 F6
Galicia, □ *Spain* 13 A1
Gällivare, *Swed.* 6 C16
Galloway, *U.K.* 10 G4
Galveston, *U.S.A.* 37 E8
Galway, *Ire.* 11 C2
Gambia, ■ *Africa* 26 F1
Gamboa, *Panama* 38 H14
Ganga, ≈ *Ind./Bangla.* 24 C4
Ganges = Ganga, ≈ *Ind./Bangla.* ...24 C4
Gaoxiong, *Taiwan* 22 D7
Garda, L. di, *Italy* 14 B4
Gascogne, □ *France* 12 E3
Gaspé, Pén de, *Canada* 35 D13
Gateshead, *U.K.* 8 C6
Gatun, *Panama* 38 H14
Gävle, *Swed.* 7 F14
Gavleborg, □ *Swed.* 7 F14
Gaza, *Israel* 25 B2
Gaziantep, *Turkey* 25 B2
Gdansk, *Poland* 17 A9
Gdynia, *Poland* 17 A9
Geelong, *Australia* 33 F7
Gelsenkirchen, *Ger.* 16 C3
Genève, *Switz.* 16 E3
Génova, *Italy* 14 B3
Gent, *Belgium* 16 C1
George Town, *Malaysia* 23 C2
Georgetown, *Guyana* 40 B7
Georgia, ■ *Asia* 18 E5
Georgia, □ *U.S.A.* 37 D10
Gera, *Ger.* 16 C6
Germany, ■ *Europe* 16 C5
Germiston, *S. Africa* 29 K5
Gerona, *Spain* 13 B7
Ghana, ■ *Africa* 26 G4
Giant's Causeway, *U.K.* 11 A5
Gibraltar, □ *Europe* 13 D3
Gibson Desert, *Australia* 32 C3
Gifu, *Japan* 21 B5
Gigha, *U.K.* 10 F3
Gijón, *Spain* 13 A3
Gillingham, *U.K.* 9 F8
Gisborne, *N.Z.* 31 H7
Gjøvik, *Norw.* 7 F11
Glasgow, *U.K.* 10 F4
Glendale, *U.S.A.* 36 D3
Glenrothes, *U.K.* 10 E5
Gliwice, *Poland* 17 C9
Głogów, *Poland* 16 C8
Gloucester, *U.K.* 9 F5
Gloucestershire, □ *U.K.* 9 F5
Goa, □ *India* 24 E3
Goiânia, *Brazil* 41 G9
Goias, □ *Brazil* 41 F9
Good Hope, C. of, *S. Africa* 29 L3
Gorkiy = Nizhniy Novgorod, *Russia* .18 D7
Gorlitz, *Ger.* 16 C7
Gosport, *U.K.* 9 G6
Göteborg, *Swed.* 7 H11
Gotland, *Swed.* 7 H15
Götaland, *Swed.* 7 G12
Gozo, *Malta* 14 F6
Grampian, □ *U.K.* 10 D6
Grampian Highlands, *U.K.* 10 E4

Gran Canaria, *Canary Is.* 26 C1
Granada, *Spain* 13 D4
Grand Bahama I., *W. Indies* 39 B9
Grand Canyon, *U.S.A.* 36 C4
Grand Cayman, *W. Indies* 39 D8
Grand Rapids, *U.S.A.* 37 B9
Grangemouth, *U.K.* 10 E5
Grantham, *U.K.* 8 E7
Gravesend, *U.K.* 9 F8
Graz, *Austria* 16 E7
Great Abaco I., *W. Indies* 39 B9
Great Australian Bight, *Australia* ...32 E4
Great Barrier Reef, *Australia* 33 B8
Great Bear L., *Canada* 34 B7
Great Divide, *Australia* 33 C8
Great Falls, *U.S.A.* 36 A4
Great Inagua I., *W. Indies* 39 C10
Great Salt Lake, *U.S.A.* 36 B4
Great Sandy Desert, *Australia* ...32 C3
Great Slave L., *Canada* 34 B8
Great Victoria Desert, *Australia* ...32 D4
Great Wall, The, *China* 22 C5
Great Yarmouth, *U.K.* 8 E9
Greater Antilles, *W. Indies* 39 D9
Greater Manchester, □ *U.K.* 8 D5
Greece, ■ *Europe* 15 E9
Green Bay, *U.S.A.* 37 B9
Greenland, ■ *N. Amer.* 4 A9
Greenock, *U.K.* 10 F4
Greensboro, *U.S.A.* 37 C11
Grenada, ■ *W. Indies* 38 Q20
Grenoble, *France* 12 D6
Gretna Green, *U.K.* 10 F5
Grey Range, *Australia* 33 D7
Grimsby, *U.K.* 8 D7
Groningen, *Neth.* 16 B3
Groot Karoo, *S. Africa* 29 L4
Groote Eylandt, *Australia* 33 A6
Gross Glockner, *Austria* 16 E6
Grudziadz, *Poland* 17 B9
Guadalajara, *Mexico* 38 C4
Guadalajara, *Spain* 13 B4
Guadarrama, Sierra de, *Spain* ...13 B4
Guadeloupe, ■ *W. Indies* 38 L20
Guadiana, ≈ *Port.* 13 D2
Guadix, *Spain* 13 D4
Guangzhou, *China* 22 D6
Guantanamo, *Cuba* 39 C9
Guatemala, ■ *Cent. Amer.* 38 D6
Guatemala City, *Guatemala* 38 E6
Guayaquil, *Ecuador* 40 D2
Guelph, *Canada* 35 D11
Guernsey, *Channel Is.* 12 B2
Guildford, *U.K.* 9 F7
Guinea, ■ *Africa* 26 F2
Guinea-Bissau, ■ *Africa* 26 F1
Guiyang, *China* 22 D5
Gujarat, □ *India* 24 D3
Gulf, The, *Asia* 25 C4
Guyana, ■ *S. Amer.* 40 B7
Guyenne, □ *France* 12 D4
Gwalior, *India* 24 C4
Gwent, □ *U.K.* 9 F4
Gwynedd, □ *U.K.* 8 E4
Györ, *Hungary* 17 E8

H

Haarlem, *Neth.* 16 B2
Hachinohe, *Japan* 21 F11
Hadrian's Wall, *U.K.* 8 C5
Hagen, *Ger.* 16 C3
Haifa, *Israel* 25 B2
Hainan Dao, *China* 22 E6
Haiti, ■ *W. Indies* 39 D10
Hakodate, *Japan* 21 F11
Halab, *Syria* 25 B2
Halberstadt, *Ger.* 16 C5
Halifax, *Canada* 35 D13
Halifax, *U.K.* 8 D6
Halland, □ *Swed.* 7 H12
Halle, *Ger.* 16 C5
Halmstad, *Swed.* 7 H12
Hamã, *Syria* 25 B2
Hamadān, *Iran* 25 B3
Hamamatsu, *Japan* 21 B5
Hamar, *Norw.* 7 F11
Hamburg, *Ger.* 16 B5
Hame, □ *Fin.* 7 F17
Hameln, *Ger.* 16 B4
Hamilton, *N.Z.* 31 G5
Hamilton, *U.K.* 10 F4
Hamilton, *Canada* 35 D11
Hamm, *Ger.* 16 C3
Hammerfest, *Norw.* 6 A17
Hammond, *U.S.A.* 37 B9
Hampshire, □ *U.K.* 9 F6
Hangzhou, *China* 22 C6
Hanoi, *Vietnam* 23 A2
Harare, *Zimbabwe* 29 H6
Harbin, *China* 22 B7
Hargeisa, *Somalia* 30 F8
Harlow, *U.K.* 9 F8
Härnösand, *Swed.* 6 E15
Harrogate, *U.K.* 8 D6
Hartlepool, *U.K.* 8 C6
Haryana, □ *India* 24 C4
Hastings, *N.Z.* 31 H6

Hastings, *U.K.* 9 G8
Haugesund, *Norw.* 7 G8
Haut Atlas, *Morocco* 26 B4
Havana = La Habana, *Cuba* 39 C8
Havant, *U.K.* 9 G7
Hawaii, *Pac. Ocean* 2 C2
Hawaii, □ *U.S.A.* 36 H16
Hawick, *U.K.* 10 F6
Hedmark, □ *Norw.* 7 F11
Hefei, *China* 22 C6
Heidelberg, *Ger.* 16 D4
Heilbronn, *Ger.* 16 D4
Helmsdale, *U.K.* 10 C5
Helsingborg, *Swed.* 7 H12
Helsingor, *Den.* 7 H12
Helsinki, *Fin.* 7 F18
Hemel Hempstead, *U.K.* 9 F7
Hengyang, *China* 22 D6
Hereford, *U.K.* 9 E5
Hereford & Worcester, □ *U.K.* 9 E5
Herford, *Ger.* 16 B4
Hermosillo, *Mexico* 38 B2
Hertfordshire, □ *U.K.* 9 F7
Hessen, □ *Ger.* 16 C4
Higashiōsaka, *Japan* 21 B4
High Wycombe, *U.K.* 9 F7
Highland, □ *U.K.* 8 D4
Hildesheim, *Ger.* 16 B4
Hilversum, *Neth.* 16 B2
Himachal Pradesh, □ *India* 24 B4
Himalaya, *Asia* 24 C5
Himeji, *Japan* 21 B4
Hims, *Syria* 25 B2
Hindu Kush, *Afghan.* 25 B5
Hirosaki, *Japan* 21 F11
Hiroshima, *Japan* 21 B3
Hobart, *Australia* 33 G8
Hohhot, *China* 22 B6
Hokkaido, *Japan* 21 F11
Holderness, *U.K.* 8 D7
Holguin, *Cuba* 39 C9
Hollywood, *U.S.A.* 36 D3
Honduras, ■ *Cent. Amer.* 38 E7
Hønefoss, *Norw.* 7 F11
Hong Kong, ■ *Asia* 22 D6
Honolulu, *Hawaii* 36 H16
Honshu, *Japan* 21 B4
Hordaland, □ *Norw.* 7 F9
Hormuz, Str. of, *Asia* 25 C4
Horn, C. = Hornos, C. de, *Chile* ...42 H3
Hornos, C. de, *Chile* 42 H3
Horsens, *Den.* 7 J10
Hospitalet, *Spain* 13 B7
Houghton-le-Spring, *U.K.* 8 C6
Houston, *U.S.A.* 37 E7
Howrah, *India* 24 D6
Hoy, *U.K.* 10 C5
Hradec Kralove, *Czech Rep.* 16 C7
Huainan, *China* 22 C6
Huang, ≈ *China* 22 C6
Huascarán, *Peru* 40 E3
Huddersfield, *U.K.* 8 D6
Hudson Bay, *Canada* 35 B11
Hudson Str., *Canada* 35 B12
Huelva, *Spain* 13 D2
Huesca, *Spain* 13 A5
Hull, *U.K.* 8 D7
Humber, ≈ *U.K.* 8 D7
Humberside, □ *U.K.* 8 D7
Hungary, ■ *Europe* 17 E9
Hunsrück, *Ger.* 16 D3
Huron, L., *N. Amer.* 37 B10
Hyderabad, *India* 24 E4
Hyderabad, *Pak.* 24 C2

I

Iaşi, *Rom.* 17 E13
Ibadan, *Nigeria* 26 G5
Ibagué, *Colombia* 40 C3
Ibiza, *Spain* 13 C6
Iceland, ■ *Europe* 6 D4
Ichinomiya, *Japan* 21 B5
Idaho, □ *U.S.A.* 36 B3
Ikaría, *Greece* 15 F12
Île-de-France, □ *France* 12 B5
Illinois, □ *U.S.A.* 37 B9
Ilorin, *Nigeria* 26 G5
Imphal, *India* 24 D7
Inch'on, *S. Korea* 22 C7
India, ■ *Asia* 24 E4
Indian Ocean, ...4 H3
Indiana, □ *U.S.A.* 37 C9
Indianapolis, *U.S.A.* 37 C9
Indonesia, ■ *Asia* 23 D3
Indore, *India* 24 D4
Indus, ≈ *Pakistan* 24 C2
Ingolstadt, *Ger.* 16 D5
Inishowen Pen., *Ire.* 11 A4
Inner Hebrides, *U.K.* 10 E3
Innsbruck, *Austria* 16 E5
Inveraray, *U.K.* 10 E3
Invercargill, *N.Z.* 31 M2
Invergordon, *U.K.* 10 D4
Inverness, *U.K.* 10 D4
Iona, *U.K.* 10 E2
Ionian Sea, *Europe* 15 E8
Iónioi Nísoi, □ *Greece* 15 E9

Iowa, □ *U.S.A.* 37 B8
Ípiros, □ *Greece* 15 E9
Ipswich, *U.K.* 9 E9
Iquique, *Chile* 40 H4
Iquitos, *Peru* 40 D4
Iráklion, *Greece* 15 G11
Iran, ■ *Asia* 25 B4
Iraq, ■ *Asia* 25 B3
Ireland, ■ *Europe* 11 C4
Irian Jaya, □ *Indonesia* 23 D5
Irish Sea, *Europe* 8 D2
Irkutsk, *Russia* 19 D11
Irrawady = Erawadi Myit, ≈ *Burma* ..24 E8
Irvine, *U.K.* 10 F4
Islay, *U.K.* 10 F2
Israel, ■ *Asia* 25 B2
Istanbul, *Turkey* 25 A1
Italy, ■ *Europe* 14 C4
Ivory Coast, ■ *Africa* 26 G3
Iwaki, *Japan* 21 G11
Iwo, *Nigeria* 26 G5
Izmir, *Turkey* 25 B1

J

Jabalpur, *India* 24 D5
Jackson, *U.S.A.* 37 D8
Jacksonville, *U.S.A.* 37 D10
Jaén, *Spain* 13 D4
Jaipur, *India* 24 C4
Jakarta, *Indonesia* 23 D2
Jamaica, ■ *W. Indies* 39 D9
James Bay, *Canada* 35 C11
Jammu & Kashmir, □ *India* 24 B3
Jämtland, □ *Norw.* 6 E13
Japan, ■ *Asia* 21 G10
Japan, Sea of, *Asia* 21 A3
Java, *Indonesia* 23 D2
Jena, *Ger.* 16 C5
Jerez, *Spain* 13 D2
Jersey, *Channel Is.* 12 B2
Jersey City, *U.S.A.* 37 B12
Jerusalem, *Israel* 25 B2
Jiddah, *S. Arabia* 25 C2
Jilin, *China* 22 B7
Jilong, *Taiwan* 22 D7
Jinan, *China* 22 C6
Jinzhou, *China* 22 B7
João Pessoa, *Brazil* 41 E12
Johannesburg, *S. Africa* 29 K5
John O'Groats, *U.K.* 10 C5
Johnstone, *U.K.* 10 F4
Jönköping, □ *Swed.* 7 H12
Jordan, ■ *Asia* 25 B2
Juàzeiro do Norte, *Brazil* 41 E11
Juiz de Fora, *Brazil* 41 H10
Jundiaí, *Brazil* 42 A7
Jura, *Europe* 12 C6
Jura, *U.K.* 10 F3

K

Kabul, *Afghan.* 25 B5
Kaduna, *Nigeria* 26 F6
Kagoshima, *Japan* 21 D2
Kaiserslautern, *Ger.* 16 D3
Kalahari, *Africa* 29 J4
Kaliningrad, *Russia* 18 D3
Kalisz, *Poland* 17 C9
Kalmar, □ *Swed.* 7 H14
Kamaishi, *Japan* 21 G11
Kampala, *Uganda* 28 D6
Kampuchea = Cambodia, ■ *Asia* ...23 B2
Kananga, *Zaïre* 28 F4
Kanazawa, *Japan* 21 A5
Kandahar, *Afghan.* 25 B5
Kangaroo I., *Australia* 33 F6
Kano, *Nigeria* 26 F6
Kanpur, *India* 24 C5
Kansas, □ *U.S.A.* 36 C7
Kansas City, *U.S.A.* 37 C8
Kaokoveld, *Namibia* 29 H2
Kaolack, *Senegal* 26 F1
Kara Sea, *Arctic* 18 B7
Karachi, *Pak.* 24 D2
Karaganda, *Kazakhstan* 18 E8
Karbalā, *Iraq* 25 B3
Kariba L., *Africa* 29 H5
Karlskrona, *Swed.* 7 H13
Karlsruhe, *Ger.* 16 D4
Karlstad, *Swed.* 7 G12
Kärnten, □ *Austria* 16 E6
Kárpathos, *Greece* 15 G12
Kāshān, *Iran* 25 B4
Kassel, *Ger.* 16 C4
Katmandu, *Nepal* 24 C6
Katowice, *Poland* 17 C9
Katsina, *Nigeria* 26 F6
Kattegat, *Scandinavia* 7 H11
Kawaguchi, *Japan* 21 B6
Kawasaki, *Japan* 21 B6
Kayseri, *Turkey* 25 B2
Kazakhstan, ■ *Asia* 18 E7
Kazan, *Russia* 18 D6
Kecskemét, *Hungary* 17 E9
Kefallinia, *Greece* 15 E9
Keflavík, *Iceland* 6 D2
Keighley, *U.K.* 8 D6
Kemān, *Iran* 25 B4

Kemi, *Fin.* 6 D18
Kenitra, *Morocco* 26 B3
Kent, □ *U.K.* 9 F8
Kentucky, □ *U.S.A.* 37 C9
Kenya, ■ *Africa* 28 D7
Kenya, Mt., *Kenya* 28 E7
Kerala, □ *India* 24 F4
Kérkira, *Greece* 15 E8
Kerry, □ *Ire.* 11 D2
Keski - Suomen, □ *Fin.* 6 E18
Key West, *U.S.A.* 37 F10
Khabarovsk, *Russia* 19 E14
Kharkov, *Ukraine* 18 E4
Khartoum = El Khartûm, *Sudan* ...27 E11
Khíos, *Greece* 15 E11
Khulna, *Bangladesh* 24 D6
Kidderminster, *U.K.* 9 E5
Kiel, *Ger.* 16 A5
Kielce, *Poland* 17 C10
Kikládhes, *Greece* 15 F11
Kikwit, *Zaïre* 28 E3
Kildare, □ *Ire.* 11 C5
Kilimanjaro, *Tanzania* 28 E7
Kilkenny, □ *Ire.* 11 D4
Killarney, *Ire.* 11 D2
Kilmarnock, *U.K.* 10 F4
Kimberley, *Australia* 32 B4
Kimberley, *S. Africa* 29 K4
King I., *Australia* 33 F7
King William I., *Canada* 34 B10
Kings Lynn, *U.K.* 8 E8
Kingston, *Jamaica* 38 J17
Kingston, *U.K.* 9 F7
Kingstown, *U.K.* 10 D4
Kinshasa, *Zaïre* 28 E3
Kintyre, *U.K.* 10 F3
Kirghizia, ■ *Asia* 18 E8
Kiribati, ■ *Pac. Ocean* 3 D18
Kirkük, *Iraq* 25 B3
Kirkcaldy, *U.K.* 10 E5
Kirkwall, *U.K.* 10 C6
Kiruna, *Swed.* 6 C15
Kisangani, *Zaïre* 28 D5
Kishinev, *Moldavia* 18 E3
Kitakyūshū, *Japan* 21 C2
Kitchener, *Canada* 35 D11
Kíthira, *Greece* 15 F10
Kitwe, *Zambia* 29 G5
Kiva, L., *Africa* 28 E5
Kiyev, *Ukraine* 18 D4
Klagenfurt, *Austria* 16 E7
Knockmealdown Mts., *Ire.* 11 D4
Knossos, *Greece* 15 G11
Knoxville, *U.S.A.* 37 C10
Kobe, *Japan* 21 B4
København, *Den.* 7 J12
Koblenz, *Ger.* 16 C3
Kōchi, *Japan* 21 C3
Kodiak I., *Alaska* 34 C4
Kolding, *Den.* 7 J10
Köln, *Ger.* 16 C3
Komsomolsk, *Russia* 19 D14
Kongsvinger, *Norw.* 7 F12
Konya, *Turkey* 25 B2
Kopervik, *Norw.* 7 G8
Kopparberg, □ *Swed.* 7 F12
Kōriyama, *Japan* 21 G11
Kos, *Greece* 15 F12
Koşice, *Slovak Rep.* 17 D10
Koskiusko, Mt., *Australia* 33 F8
Kosovo, □ *Yug.* 15 C9
Kowloon, *Hong Kong* 22 D6
Kraków, *Poland* 17 C9
Krasnodar, *Russia* 18 E4
Krasnoyarsk, *Russia* 19 D10
Krefeld, *Ger.* 16 C3
Kristiansand, *Norw.* 7 G10
Kristianstad, □ *Swed.* 7 J13
Kristiansund, *Norw.* 6 E10
Kriti, *Greece* 15 G11
Krivoy Rog, *Ukraine* 18 E4
Kronoberg, □ *Swed.* 7 H13
Kuala Lumpur, *Malaysia* 23 C2
Kumamoto, *Japan* 21 C2
Kumasi, *Ghana* 26 G4
Kuopio, □ *Fin.* 6 E19
Kurashiki, *Japan* 21 B3
Kure, *Japan* 21 B3
Kurilskiye Ostrova, *Russia* 19 E16
Kushiro, *Japan* 21 F11
Kuwait, ■ *Asia* 25 C3
Kuybyshev = Samara, *Russia* 18 D6
Kwangju, *S. Korea* 22 C7
Kyūshū, *Japan* 21 C2
Kyle of Lochalsh, *U.K.* 10 D3
Kyoga, L., *Uganda* 28 D6
Kyōto, *Japan* 21 B4
Kyyiv = Kiev, *Ukraine* 18 D4

L

La Boca, *Panama* 38 H14
La Chorrera, *Panama* 38 H14
La Coruña, *Spain* 13 A1
La Habana, *Cuba* 39 C8
La Paz, *Bolivia* 40 G5
La Plata, *Argentina* 42 D5
La Rioja, □ *Spain* 13 A4
La Rochelle, *France* 12 C3

La Spézia, Italy ...14 B3
Labrador, Coast of, Canada ...35 C13
Ladozhskoye, Ozero, Russia ...18 C4
Lagos, Port. ...13 D1
Lagos, Nigeria ...26 G5
Lahore, Pak. ...24 B3
Lahti, Fin. ...7 F18
Lakshadweep Is., India ...24 F3
Lancashire, □ U.K. ...8 D5
Lancaster, U.K. ...8 C5
Lancaster Sd., Canada ...35 A11
Landskrona, Swed. ...7 J12
Languedoc, □ France ...12 E5
Lansing, U.S.A. ...37 B10
Lanzhou, China ...22 C5
Laois, □ Ire. ...11 D4
Laos, ■ Asia ...23 B2
Lapi, □ Fin. ...6 C19
Lappland, Fin. ...6 B18
Laptev Sea, Arctic ...19 B13
Laredo, U.S.A. ...36 E7
Lárisa, Greece ...15 E10
Larne, □ U.K. ...11 B6
Las Palmas, Canary Is. ...26 C1
Las Vegas, U.S.A. ...36 C3
Latvia, ■ Europe ...18 D3
Lauchhammer, Ger. ...16 C6
Launceston, Australia ...33 G8
Lausanne, Switz. ...16 E3
Lawton, U.S.A. ...36 D7
Le Havre, France ...12 B4
Le Mans, France ...12 B4
Le Moule, Guadeloupe ...38 L20
Leamington, U.K. ...9 E6
Lebanon, ■ Asia ...25 B2
Lecce, Italy ...15 D8
Leeds, U.K. ...8 D6
Leeuwarden, Neth. ...16 B2
Leeward Is., W. Indies ...39 D12
Legnica, Poland ...16 C8
Leicester, U.K. ...9 E6
Leicestershire, □ U.K. ...9 E6
Leiden, Neth. ...16 B2
Leinster, Ire. ...11 C4
Leipzig, Ger. ...16 C6
Leith, U.K. ...10 F5
Leitrim, □ Ire. ...11 B3
Lena, ≈ Russia ...19 B13
Leningrad = St. Peterburg, Russia ..18 D4
León, Mexico ...38 C4
León, Spain ...13 A3
Lérida, Spain ...13 B6
Lesotho, ■ Africa ...29 K5
Lesser Antilles, W. Indies ...39 E12
Lésvos, Greece ...15 E11
Letchworth, U.K. ...9 F7
Lethbridge, Canada ...34 D8
Leuven, Belgium ...16 C2
Levkás, Greece ...15 E9
Levkôsia, Cyprus ...25 B2
Lewis, U.K. ...10 C2
Lhasa, China ...22 D4
Lianyungang, China ...22 C6
Liberec, Czech. Rep. ...16 C7
Liberia, ■ Africa ...26 G3
Lîbîya, Sahrâ', Africa ...27 C9
Libreville, Gabon ...28 D1
Libya, ■ Africa ...27 C8
Liechtenstein, ■ Europe ...16 E4
Liège, Belgium ...16 C2
Liffey, ≈ Ire. ...11 C5
Liguria, □ Italy ...14 B3
Ligurian Sea, Italy ...14 C3
Likasi, Zaïre ...28 G5
Lille, France ...12 A5
Lillehammer, Norw. ...7 F11
Lilongwe, Malawi ...29 G6
Lima, Peru ...40 F3
Limavady, U.K. ...11 A5
Limerick, Ire. ...11 D3
Límnos, Greece ...15 E11
Limoges, France ...12 C4
Limousin, □ France ...12 D4
Limpopo, ≈ Africa ...29 K6
Linares, Spain ...13 C4
Lincoln, U.S.A. ...37 B7
Lincoln, U.K. ...8 D7
Lincolnshire, □ U.K. ...8 D7
Linköping, Swed. ...7 G13
Linz, Austria ...16 D7
Lisboa, Port. ...13 C1
Lisburn, U.K. ...11 B5
Listowel, Ire. ...11 D2
Lithuania, ■ Europe ...18 D3
Little Minch, U.K. ...10 D2
Little Rock, U.S.A. ...37 D8
Liverpool, U.K. ...8 D5
Livingston, U.K. ...10 F5
Livingstone, Zambia ...29 H5
Livorno, Italy ...14 C4
Lizard, U.K. ...9 H2
Ljubljana, Slovenia ...14 A6
Llanelli, U.K. ...9 F3
Lloret, Spain ...13 B7
Lobito, Angola ...29 G2
Locarno, L. di, Italy ...14 A3
Lochaber, U.K. ...10 E3
Lockerbie, U.K. ...10 F5
Łódź, Poland ...17 C9

Lofoten, Norw. ...6 B12
Logroño, Spain ...13 A4
Loire, ≈ France ...12 C2
Lolland, Den. ...7 J11
Lombardia, □ Italy ...14 B3
Lombok, Indonesia ...23 D3
Lomé, Togo ...26 G5
Lomond, L., U.K. ...10 E4
Łomza, Poland ...17 B10
London, U.K. ...9 F7
London, Canada ...35 D11
Londonderry, U.K. ...11 B4
Londrina, Brazil ...42 A6
Long Beach, U.S.A. ...36 D3
Long Island, U.S.A. ...37 B12
Longford, □ Ire. ...11 C4
Lorca, Spain ...13 D5
Lorne, U.K. ...10 E3
Lorraine, □ France ...12 B7
Los Angeles, U.S.A. ...36 D3
Lothian, □ U.K. ...10 F5
Loughborough, U.K. ...8 E6
Louisiana, □ U.S.A. ...37 D8
Louisville, U.S.A. ...37 C9
Lourdes, France ...12 E3
Louth, □ Ire. ...11 C5
Lower Hutt, N.Z. ...31 J5
Lowestoft, U.K. ...9 E9
Luanda, Angola ...28 F2
Luanshya, Zambia ...29 G5
Lubbock, U.S.A. ...36 D6
Lübeck, Ger. ...16 B5
Lublin, Poland ...17 C11
Lubumbashi, Zaïre ...29 G5
Lucca, Italy ...14 C4
Lucknow, India ...24 C5
Ludwigshafen, Ger. ...16 D4
Lugano, Switz. ...16 E5
Lugo, Spain ...13 A2
Luleå, Swed. ...6 D17
Lüneburger Heide, Ger. ...16 B5
Luoyang, China ...22 C6
Lurgan, U.K. ...11 B5
Lusaka, Zambia ...29 H5
Luton, U.K. ...9 F7
Luxembourg, ■ Europe ...16 D3
Luzern, Switz. ...16 E4
Luzhou, China ...22 D5
Luzon, Philippines ...23 B4
Lvov, Ukraine ...18 E3
Lycksele, Swed. ...6 D15
Lymington, U.K. ...9 G6
Lyon, France ...12 D6

M
M'Clintock Chan., Canada ...34 B9
Macapá, Brazil ...41 C8
Macau, ■ Asia ...22 D6
Macclesfield, U.K. ...8 D5
Macdonnell Ranges, Australia ...32 C5
Macedonia, ■ Europe ...15 D9
Maceió, Brazil ...41 E11
Mackenzie, ≈ Canada ...34 B6
Mackenzie Mts., Canada ...34 B6
Macroom, Ire. ...11 E3
Madagascar, ■ Africa ...29 J9
Madeira, Atl. Ocean ...26 B1
Madeira, ≈ S. Amer. ...40 E6
Madhya Pradesh, □ India ...24 D4
Madison, U.S.A. ...37 B9
Madras, India ...24 F5
Madre, L., Mexico ...38 B5
Madrid, □ Spain ...13 B4
Madrid, Spain ...13 B4
Madurai, India ...24 G4
Maebashi, Japan ...21 A6
Mafia I., Tanzania ...28 F7
Magadan, Russia ...19 D16
Magalluf, Spain ...13 C7
Magdeburg, Ger. ...16 B6
Magherafelt, □ U.K. ...11 B5
Maharashtra, □ India ...24 D4
Mahon, Spain ...13 C8
Mai-Ndombe, L., Zaïre ...28 E3
Maidenhead, U.K. ...9 F7
Maidstone, U.K. ...9 F8
Maiduguri, Nigeria ...27 F7
Maimana, Afghan. ...25 B5
Maine, □ France ...12 B3
Maine, □ U.S.A. ...37 A13
Mainz, Ger. ...16 D4
Makasar = Ujung Pandang, Indonesia ...23 D3
Makedhona, □ Greece ...15 D10
Makgadikgadi Salt Pans, Botswana 29 J5
Makkah, S. Arabia ...25 C3
Malaga, Spain ...13 D3
Malatya, Turkey ...25 B2
Malawi, ■ Africa ...29 G6
Malaysia, ■ Asia ...23 C2
Maldives, ■ Ind. Ocean ...24 G3
Mali, ■ Africa ...26 E4
Mallorca, Spain ...13 C7
Mallow, Ire. ...11 D3
Malmö, Swed. ...7 J12
Malmöhus, □ Swed. ...7 J12
Malta, ■ Europe ...14 G6
Malvern Hills, U.K. ...9 E5
Man, I. of, U.K. ...8 C3

Managua, Nicaragua ...38 E7
Manaus, Brazil ...40 D6
Manchester, U.K. ...8 D5
Mandalay, Burma ...24 D8
Manila, Philippines ...23 B4
Manitoba, □ Canada ...34 C10
Manitoba, L., Canada ...34 C10
Manizales, Colombia ...40 B3
Mannheim, Ger. ...16 D4
Mansel I., Canada ...35 B11
Mansfield, U.K. ...8 D6
Mantova, Italy ...14 B4
Maputo, Mozambique ...29 K6
Mar del Plata, Argentina ...42 D5
Maracaibo, Venezuela ...40 A4
Maracay, Venezuela ...40 A5
Marajó, I. de, Brazil ...41 D9
Maranhão, □ Brazil ...41 E9
Marbella, Spain ...13 D3
Marche, □ France ...12 C4
Marche, □ Italy ...14 C5
Margate, U.K. ...9 F9
Mariana Is., Pac. Ocean ...3 D17
Marie-Galante, W. Indies ...38 M20
Marília, Brazil ...41 H8
Maringá, Brazil ...41 A6
Marmara, Sea of, Turkey ...25 A1
Marquesas Is., Pac. Ocean ...2 E2
Marrakech, Morocco ...26 B3
Marseille, France ...12 E6
Marshall Is., ■ Pac. Ocean ...3 D18
Martha's Vineyard, U.S.A. ...37 B12
Martinique, □ W. Indies ...38 N21
Maryland, □ U.S.A. ...37 C11
Massachusetts, □ U.S.A. ...37 B12
Massif Central, France ...12 D5
Matadi, Zaïre ...28 F2
Matamoros, Mexico ...38 B5
Mato Grosso, □ Brazil ...41 F7
Mato Grosso do Sul, □ Brazil ...41 G7
Matsuyama, Japan ...21 C3
Matterhorn, Switz. ...16 E3
Maturín, Venezuela ...40 B6
Mauritania, ■ Africa ...26 E2
Mauritius, ■ Ind. Ocean ...30 H9
Mayo, □ Ire. ...11 C2
Mazar-i-Sharif, Afghan. ...25 B5
Mbandaka, Zaïre ...28 D3
Meath, □ Ire. ...11 C5
Mecca = Makkah, S. Arabia ...25 C2
Mechelen, Belgium ...16 C2
Medan, Indonesia ...23 C1
Medellín, Colombia ...40 B3
Medicine Hat, Canada ...34 D8
Medina = Al Madinah, S. Arabia ...25 C2
Mediterranean Sea, ...5 H7
Meerut, India ...24 C4
Meknès, Morocco ...26 B3
Mekong, ≈ Asia ...23 B2
Melbourne, Australia ...33 F8
Melrose, U.K. ...10 F6
Melville Is., Australia ...32 A5
Memphis, U.S.A. ...37 C9
Menai Strait, U.K. ...8 D3
Mendip Hills, U.K. ...9 F5
Mendoza, Argentina ...42 C3
Menorca, Spain ...13 B7
Mentawai Is., Indonesia ...23 D1
Merca, Somalia ...30 F8
Mérida, Mexico ...38 C7
Mersey, ≈ U.K. ...8 D5
Merseyside, □ U.K. ...8 D4
Merthyr Tydfil, U.K. ...9 F4
Messina, Italy ...14 E6
Metz, France ...12 B7
Mexicali, Mexico ...38 A1
Mexico, ■ Cent. Amer. ...38 B3
Mexico City, Mexico ...38 D5
Mexico, G. de, Cent. Amer. ...38 B6
Miami, U.S.A. ...37 E10
Michigan, □ U.S.A. ...37 A9
Michigan, L., U.S.A. ...37 B9
Micronesia, ■ Pac. Ocean ...3 D17
Mid Glamorgan, □ U.K. ...9 F4
Middlesbrough, U.K. ...8 C6
Midland, U.S.A. ...36 D6
Mikkeli, □ Fin. ...6 E19
Milano, Italy ...14 B3
Milton Keynes, U.K. ...9 E7
Milwaukee, U.S.A. ...37 B9
Minas Gerais, □ Brazil ...41 G9
Mindanao, Philippines ...23 C4
Minneapolis, U.S.A. ...37 B8
Minnesota, □ U.S.A. ...37 A8
Minsk, Belorussia ...18 D3
Miskolc, Hungary ...17 D10
Misrätah, Libya ...27 B8
Mississippi, □ U.S.A. ...37 D9
Mississippi, ≈ U.S.A. ...37 E9
Missouri, □ U.S.A. ...37 C8
Missouri, ≈ U.S.A. ...37 C8
Miyako, Japan ...21 G11
Mobile, U.S.A. ...37 D9
Mobutu, L., Africa ...28 D6
Moçambique, Mozambique ...29 H8
Módena, Italy ...14 B4

Mogadishu, Somalia ...30 E8
Moldavia, ■ Europe ...18 E3
Molise, □ Italy ...14 D6
Mölndal, Swed. ...7 H12
Moluccas, Indonesia ...23 C4
Mombasa, Kenya ...28 E7
Mona, Canal de la, W. Indies ...39 D11
Monaco, ■ Europe ...12 E7
Monaghan, □ Ire. ...11 B5
Mönchengladbach, Ger. ...16 C3
Moncton, Canada ...35 D13
Mongolia, ■ Asia ...22 B5
Monrovia, Liberia ...26 G2
Mont St. - Michel, France ...12 B3
Montana, □ U.S.A. ...36 A4
Monte Carlo, Monaco ...12 E7
Montego Bay, Jamaica ...38 J16
Montenegro, □ Yug. ...15 C8
Monterrey, Mexico ...38 B4
Montes Claros, Brazil ...41 G10
Montevideo, Uruguay ...42 C5
Montgomery, U.S.A. ...37 D9
Montpellier, France ...12 E5
Montréal, Canada ...35 D12
Montrose, U.K. ...10 E6
Montserrat, W. Indies ...38 L19
Moray Firth, U.K. ...10 D5
More og Romsdal, □ Norw. ...6 E9
Morecambe B., U.K. ...8 C4
Morelia, Mexico ...38 D4
Morena, Sierra, Spain ...13 C3
Morioka, Japan ...21 G11
Morocco, ■ Africa ...26 B3
Morvern, U.K. ...10 E3
Moscow = Moskva, Russia ...18 D4
Mosel, ≈ Ger. ...16 C3
Moskva, Russia ...18 D4
Mostaganem, Algeria ...26 A5
Motala, Swed. ...7 G13
Motherwell, U.K. ...10 F5
Moulmyaing, Burma ...24 E8
Mourne Mts., U.K. ...11 B5
Mozambique, ■ Africa ...29 J6
Mozambique Chan., Africa ...29 H8
Muck, U.K. ...10 E2
Mufulira, Zambia ...29 G5
Mülheim, Ger. ...16 C3
Mulhouse, France ...12 C7
Mull, U.K. ...10 E3
Mullet Pen., Ire. ...11 B1
Mullingar, Ire. ...11 C4
Multan, Pak. ...24 B3
München, Ger. ...16 D5
Munich = München, Ger. ...16 D5
Munster, Ire. ...11 D3
Münster, Ger. ...16 C3
Murcia, □ Spain ...13 C5
Murcia, Spain ...13 C5
Murmansk, Russia ...18 C4
Muroran, Japan ...21 F11
Murray River, ≈ Australia ...33 F6
Murray River Basin, Australia ...33 E7
Musgrave Ranges, Australia ...32 D5
Mustique, W. Indies ...38 Q20
Mwanza, Tanzania ...28 E6
Myanmar = Burma, ■ Asia ...24 D8
Mysore, India ...24 F4

N
Nagano, Japan ...21 A6
Nagaoka, Japan ...21 G10
Nagasaki, Japan ...21 C1
Nagoya, Japan ...21 B5
Nagpur, India ...24 D4
Nairobi, Kenya ...28 E7
Nakhodka, Russia ...19 E14
Namaland, Namibia ...29 J3
Namibia, ■ Africa ...29 J3
Namibwoestyn, Namibia ...29 J2
Namsos, Norw. ...6 D11
Nanchang, China ...22 D6
Nancy, France ...12 B7
Nanjing, China ...22 C6
Nanning, China ...22 D5
Nansei-Shoto, Japan ...21 J8
Nantes, France ...12 C3
Napier, N.Z. ...31 H6
Napoli, Italy ...14 D6
Narbonne, France ...12 E5
Narvik, Norw. ...6 B14
Naser, Buheiret en, Egypt ...27 D11
Nashville, U.S.A. ...37 C9
Nassau, Bahamas ...39 B9
Natal, □ S. Africa ...29 K6
Natal, Brazil ...41 E11
Nauru, ■ Pac. Ocean ...3 E18
Navarra, □ Spain ...13 A5
Náxos, Greece ...15 F11
Ndjamena, Chad ...27 F8
Ndola, Zambia ...29 G5
Nebraska, □ U.S.A. ...36 B6
Negro, ≈ Brazil ...40 D6
Neiva, Colombia ...40 C3
Nemuro, Japan ...21 F12
Nemuro-Kaikyō, Japan ...21 F12
Nepal, ■ Asia ...24 C5
Ness, L., U.K. ...10 D4

Netherlands, ■ Europe ...16 B2
Nevada, □ U.S.A. ...36 C3
Nevers, France ...12 C5
New Bedford, U.S.A. ...37 B12
New Britain, Pac. Ocean ...3 E17
New Brunswick, □ Canada ...35 D13
New Caledonia, Pac. Ocean ...3 F18
New Forest, U.K. ...9 G6
New Hampshire, □ U.S.A. ...37 B12
New Haven, U.S.A. ...37 B12
New Jersey, □ U.S.A. ...37 C12
New Mexico, □ U.S.A. ...36 D5
New Orleans, U.S.A. ...37 E9
New Plymouth, N.Z. ...31 H5
New Providence I., W. Indies ...39 B9
New South Wales, □ Australia ...33 E8
New York, U.S.A. ...37 B12
New York, □ U.S.A. ...37 B11
New Zealand, ■ Pac. Ocean ...31 J5
Newark, U.S.A. ...37 B12
Newbury, U.K. ...9 F6
Newcastle, Australia ...33 E9
Newcastle, U.K. ...8 C6
Newcastle-under-Lyme, U.K. ...8 D5
Newfoundland, □ Canada ...35 C14
Newport, U.K. ...9 F5
Newport News, U.S.A. ...37 C11
Newquay, U.K. ...9 G2
Newry, U.K. ...11 B5
Newtownabbey, □ U.K. ...11 B6
Newtownards, U.K. ...11 B6
Niagara Falls, N. Amer. ...35 D12
Niamey, Niger ...26 F5
Nicaragua, ■ Cent. Amer. ...38 E7
Nice, France ...12 E7
Nicobar Is., India ...24 G7
Niederösterreich, □ Austria ...16 D7
Niedersachsen, □ Ger. ...16 B4
Niger, ■ Africa ...26 E6
Niger, ≈ Africa ...26 G6
Nigeria, ■ Africa ...26 G6
Niigata, Japan ...21 G10
Nijmegen, Neth. ...16 C2
Nîl el Abyad, ≈ Africa ...27 E11
Nîl el Azraq, ≈ Africa ...27 E11
Nîl, Nahr en, ≈ Africa ...27 C11
Nile = Nîl, Nahr en, ≈ Africa ...27 C11
Nîmes, France ...12 E6
Ningbo, China ...22 D7
Nishinomiya, Japan ...21 B4
Niteroi, Brazil ...41 H10
Nizhniy Novgorod, Russia ...18 D5
Nord-Trondelag, □ Norw. ...6 D12
Nordland, □ Norw. ...6 C13
Nordrhein - Westfalen, □ Ger. ...16 C3
Norfolk, □ U.S.A. ...37 C11
Norfolk, □ U.K. ...8 E8
Normandie, □ France ...12 B3
Norrbotten, □ Norw. ...6 C15
Norrköping, Swed. ...7 G13
North Carolina, □ U.S.A. ...37 C11
North Channel, Europe ...8 C3
North Dakota, □ U.S.A. ...36 A6
North Downs, U.K. ...9 F7
North Island, N.Z. ...31 H5
North Korea, ■ Asia ...22 B7
North Minch, U.K. ...10 C3
North Sea, Europe ...8 C6
North Uist, U.K. ...10 D1
North West Highlands, U.K. ...10 D3
North West Territories, □ Canada ...34 B8
North Yorkshire, □ U.K. ...8 C6
North Yorkshire Moors, U.K. ...8 C7
Northampton, U.K. ...9 E7
Northamptonshire, □ U.K. ...9 E7
Northern Ireland, □ U.K. ...11 B4
Northern Territory, □ Australia ...32 B5
Northumberland, □ U.K. ...8 B5
Norway, ■ Europe ...6 E11
Norwegian Sea, Atl. Ocean ...4 C8
Norwich, U.K. ...8 E9
Nottingham, U.K. ...8 E6
Nottinghamshire, □ U.K. ...8 D6
Nouakchott, Mauritania ...26 E1
Nova Scotia, □ Canada ...35 D13
Novaya Zemlya, Russia ...18 B6
Novi Sad, Yug. ...15 B8
Novokuznetsk, Russia ...18 D9
Novosibirsk, Russia ...18 D9
Novosibirskiye Ostrova, Russia ...19 B13
Nûbîya, Es Sahrâ en, Sudan ...27 D11
Nullarbor Plain, Australia ...32 E4
Nuneaton, U.K. ...9 E6
Nunivak I., Alaska ...34 B3
Nürnberg, Ger. ...16 D5
Nyasa, L., Africa ...29 G6
Nykøbing, Den. ...7 J11

O
Oakland, U.S.A. ...36 C2
Ob, ≈ Russia ...18 C7
Oban, U.K. ...10 E3
Oberhausen, Ger. ...16 C3
Oberösterreich, □ Austria ...16 D6
Obihiro, Japan ...21 F11
Odense, Den. ...7 J11
Oder, ≈ Europe ...16 B7

Odessa, *Ukraine* ...18 E4
Odessa, *U.S.A.* ...36 D6
Offaly, □ *Ire.* ...11 C4
Offenbach, *Ger.* ...16 C4
Ogbomosho, *Nigeria* ...26 G5
Ogden, *U.S.A.* ...36 B4
Ohio, ≈ *U.S.A.* ...37 C9
Ohio, □ *U.S.A.* ...37 B10
Okavango Swamps, *Botswana* ...29 H4
Okayama, *Japan* ...21 B3
Okazaki, *Japan* ...21 B5
Okhotsk, *Russia* ...19 D15
Okhotsk Sea of, *Arctic* ...19 D15
Oki-Shotō, *Japan* ...21 A3
Oklahoma, □ *U.S.A.* ...37 C7
Oklahoma City, *U.S.A.* ...37 C7
Okushiri-Tō, *Japan* ...21 F10
Öland, *Swed.* ...7 H14
Oldenburg, *Ger.* ...16 B4
Oldham, *U.K.* ...8 D5
Olimbos, *Greece* ...15 D10
Olomouc, *Czech Rep.* ...16 D8
Olympia, *Greece* ...15 F9
Omagh, *U.K.* ...11 B4
Omaha, *U.S.A.* ...37 B7
Oman, ■ *Asia* ...25 C4
Oman, Gulf of, *Asia* ...25 C4
Omdurmân, *Sudan* ...27 E11
Omsk, *Russia* ...18 D8
Ōmuta, *Japan* ...21 C2
Onezhskoye, Ozero, *Russia* ...18 C4
Onitsha, *Nigeria* ...26 G6
Ontario, □ *Canada* ...35 C11
Ontario, L., *N. Amer.* ...35 D12
Opava, *Czech Rep.* ...17 D8
Oppland, □ *Norw.* ...7 F10
Oradea, *Rom.* ...17 E10
Oran, *Algeria* ...26 A4
Oranje, ≈ *S. Africa* ...29 K3
Oranje-Vrystaat, □ *S. Africa* ...29 K5
Örebro, □ *Swed.* ...7 G13
Oregon, □ *U.S.A.* ...36 B2
Orense, *Spain* ...13 A2
Orinoco, ≈ *S. Amer.* ...40 B6
Orissa, □ *India* ...24 D5
Orkney, □ *U.K.* ...10 B5
Orlando, *U.S.A.* ...37 E10
Orleanais, □ *France* ...12 C4
Orleans, *France* ...12 C4
Orumiyeh, *Iran* ...25 B3
Oruro, *Bolivia* ...40 G5
Ōsaka, *Japan* ...21 B4
Oshawa, *Canada* ...35 D12
Oshogbo, *Nigeria* ...26 G5
Osijek, *Croatia* ...15 B8
Oskarshamn, *Swed.* ...7 H14
Oslo, *Norw.* ...7 G11
Osnabrück, *Ger.* ...16 B4
Östersund, *Swed.* ...6 E13
Ostfriesische Inseln, *Ger.* ...16 B3
Ostrava, *Czech Rep.* ...17 D9
Ostrov Vrangelya, *Russia* ...19 B18
Otaru, *Japan* ...21 F11
Otranto, Str. of, *Italy* ...15 D8
Ottawa, *Canada* ...35 D12
Öttztal, *Austria* ...16 E5
Ouagadougou, *Burkina Faso* ...26 F4
Oujda, *Morocco* ...26 B4
Oulu, *Fin.* ...6 D18
Outer Hebrides, *U.K.* ...10 D1
Oviedo, *Spain* ...13 A3
Owambo, *Namibia* ...29 H3
Ox Mts., *Ire.* ...11 B3
Oxford, *U.K.* ...9 F6
Oxfordshire, □ *U.K.* ...9 F6

P

Pacaraima, Sierra, *S. Amer.* ...40 C6
Pacific Ocean, ...2 D3
Padang, *Indonesia* ...23 D2
Pádova, *Italy* ...14 B4
Paisley, *U.K.* ...10 F4
Pakistan, ■ *Asia* ...24 C2
Palawan, *Philippines* ...23 B3
Palembang, *Indonesia* ...23 D2
Palencia, *Spain* ...13 A3
Palermo, *Italy* ...14 E5
Palma, *Spain* ...13 C7
Palmerston North, *N.Z.* ...31 J5
Palmira, *Colombia* ...40 C3
Pamplona, *Spain* ...13 A5
Panama, ■ *Cent. Amer.* ...39 F8
Panama Canal, *Panama* ...38 H14
Panama City, *Panama* ...39 H14
Panama, G. de, *Panama* ...39 F9
Papua New Guinea, ■ *Pac. Ocean* ...3 E17
Pará, □ *Brazil* ...41 D8
Paraguay, ■ *S. Amer.* ...42 A5
Paraíba, □ *Brazil* ...41 E11
Paramaribo, *Surinam* ...41 B7
Parana, ≈ *S. Amer.* ...42 C4
Paraná, □ *Brazil* ...42 A6
Paraná, *Argentina* ...42 C4
Parecis, Serra dos, *Brazil* ...40 F6
Paris, *France* ...12 B5
Parma, *Italy* ...14 B4

Pasadena, *U.S.A.* ...36 D3
Pasto, *Colombia* ...40 C3
Patna, *India* ...24 C6
Patos L. dos, *Brazil* ...42 C6
Patrai, *Greece* ...15 E9
Pavia, *Italy* ...14 B3
Pecs, *Hungary* ...17 E9
Peking = Beijing, *China* ...22 C6
Pelopónnisos, □ *Greece* ...15 F10
Pelotas, *Brazil* ...42 C6
Pemba I., *Tanzania* ...28 F7
Pennine Range, *U.K.* ...8 C5
Pennsylvania, □ *U.S.A.* ...37 B11
Pentland Firth, *U.K.* ...10 C5
Penzance, *U.K.* ...9 G2
Peoria, *U.S.A.* ...37 B9
Pereira, *Colombia* ...40 C3
Perm, *Russia* ...18 D6
Pernambuco, □ *Brazil* ...41 E11
Perpignan, *France* ...12 E5
Perth, *Australia* ...32 E2
Perth, *U.K.* ...10 E5
Peru, ■ *S. Amer.* ...40 E3
Perúgia, *Italy* ...14 C5
Pésaro, *Italy* ...14 C5
Pescara, *Italy* ...14 C6
Peshawar, *Pak.* ...24 B3
Peterboro', *Canada* ...35 D12
Peterborough, *U.K.* ...9 E7
Peterhead, *U.K.* ...10 D7
Petropavlovsk-Kamchatskiy, *Russia* 19 D16
Petrópolis, *Brazil* ...41 H10
Pforzheim, *Ger.* ...16 D4
Phanh Bho Ho Chi Minh, *Vietnam* ...23 B2
Philadelphia, *U.S.A.* ...37 B12
Philippi, *Greece* ...15 D11
Philippines, ■ *Asia* ...23 B4
Phnom Penh, *Cambodia* ...23 B2
Phoenix, *U.S.A.* ...36 D4
Phoenix Is., *Pac. Ocean* ...2 E1
Piacenza, *Italy* ...14 B3
Piauí, □ *Brazil* ...41 E10
Picardie, □ *France* ...12 A5
Piemonte, □ *Italy* ...14 B2
Pietermaritzburg, *S. Africa* ...29 K6
Pindos Oros, *Greece* ...15 E9
Piotrków Trybunalsk, *Poland* ...17 C9
Piracicaba, *Brazil* ...41 H9
Piraievs, *Greece* ...15 F10
Pisa, *Italy* ...14 C4
Pistóia, *Italy* ...14 C4
Piteå, *Swed.* ...6 D16
Pittsburgh, *U.S.A.* ...37 B11
Plauen, *Ger.* ...16 C6
Pleven, *Bulg.* ...15 C11
Ploiești, *Rom.* ...17 F13
Plovdiv, *Bulg.* ...15 C11
Plymouth, *U.K.* ...9 G3
Plzeň, *Czech Rep.* ...16 D6
Po, ≈ *Italy* ...14 B5
Podgorica, *Yug.* ...15 C8
Pointe Noire, *Congo* ...28 E2
Pointe-à Pitre, *Guadeloupe* ...38 L20
Poitou, □ *France* ...12 C3
Poland, ■ *Europe* ...17 C9
Ponce, *Puerto Rico* ...39 D11
Pondicherry, *India* ...24 F4
Ponta Grossa, *Brazil* ...42 B6
Pontefract, *U.K.* ...8 D6
Pontevedra, *Spain* ...13 A1
Pontiac, *U.S.A.* ...37 B10
Pontypool, *U.K.* ...9 F4
Pontypridd, *U.K.* ...9 F4
Poole, *U.K.* ...9 G6
Poona = Pune, *India* ...24 E3
Poopó, L., *Bolivia* ...40 G5
Popocatepetl, *Mexico* ...38 D5
Pori, *Fin.* ...7 F16
Port au Prince, *Haiti* ...39 D10
Port Elizabeth, *S. Africa* ...29 L5
Port Glasgow, *U.K.* ...10 F4
Port Harcourt, *Nigeria* ...26 H6
Port Laoise, *Ire.* ...11 C4
Port of Spain, *Trinidad* ...38 S20
Port Said = Bûr Saîd, *Egypt* ...27 B11
Port Talbot, *U.K.* ...9 F4
Portland, *U.S.A.* ...36 A2
Porto, *Port.* ...13 B1
Pôrto Alegre, *Brazil* ...42 C6
Portree, *U.K.* ...10 D2
Portsmouth, *U.K.* ...9 G6
Portsmouth, *U.S.A.* ...37 C11
Portugal, ■ *Europe* ...13 C1
Potosí, *Bolivia* ...40 G5
Potsdam, *Ger.* ...16 B6
Powys, □ *U.K.* ...9 E4
Poznan, *Poland* ...16 B8
Prague = Praha, *Czech Rep.* ...16 C7
Praha, *Czech Rep.* ...16 C7
Prato, *Italy* ...14 C4
Preston, *U.K.* ...8 D5
Pretoria, *S. Africa* ...29 K5
Prince Albert, *Canada* ...34 C9
Prince Charles I., *Canada* ...35 B12
Prince Edward I., □ *Canada* ...35 D13
Prince of Wales I., *Alaska* ...34 C6
Prince of Wales I., □ *Canada* ...34 A10
Provence, □ *France* ...12 E6
Providence, *U.S.A.* ...37 B12

Puebla, *Mexico* ...38 D5
Pueblo, *U.S.A.* ...36 C6
Puerto Rico, ≈ *W. Indies* ...39 D11
Puglia, □ *Italy* ...14 D7
Pula, *Croatia* ...14 B5
Pune, *India* ...24 E3
Punjab, □ *India* ...24 B4
Purbeck, I. of, *U.K.* ...9 G5
Pusan, *S. Korea* ...22 C7
Pyongyang, *N. Korea* ...22 C7
Pyrenées, *France* ...12 E4

Q

Qatar, ■ *Asia* ...25 C4
Qingdao, *China* ...22 C7
Qiqihar, *China* ...22 B7
Quantock Hills, *U.K.* ...9 F4
Quebec, □ *Canada* ...35 C13
Quebec, *Canada* ...35 D12
Queen Charlotte Is., *Canada* ...34 C6
Queen Maud Gulf, *Canada* ...34 B9
Queensland, □ *Australia* ...33 C7
Quezon City, *Philippines* ...23 B4
Quito, *Ecuador,* ...40 D3

R

Rabat, *Morocco* ...26 B3
Radom, *Poland* ...17 C10
Ragusa, *Italy* ...14 F6
Rajasthan, □ *India* ...24 C3
Ramsgate, *U.K.* ...9 F9
Randers, *Den.* ...7 H11
Rangoon, *Burma* ...24 E8
Rasht, *Iran* ...25 B3
Rathlin I., *U.K.* ...11 A5
Rauma, *Fin.* ...7 F16
Ravenna, *Italy* ...14 B5
Rawalpindi, *Pak.* ...24 B3
Reading, *U.K.* ...9 F7
Rebun-Tō, *Japan* ...21 E11
Recife, *Brazil* ...41 E12
Red River, ≈ *U.S.A.* ...37 D8
Red Sea, *Asia* ...25 C2
Redditch, *U.K.* ...9 E6
Regensburg, *Ger.* ...16 D6
Réggio di Calábria, *Italy* ...14 E6
Réggio nell'Emilia, *Italy* ...14 B4
Regina, *Canada* ...34 C9
Reichenbach, *Ger.* ...16 C6
Reigate, *U.K.* ...9 F7
Reims, *France* ...12 B6
Reina Adelaida, Arch., *Chile* ...42 G2
Reindeer L., *Canada* ...34 C9
Remscheid, *Ger.* ...16 C3
Rennes, *France* ...12 B3
Reno, *U.S.A.* ...36 C3
Réunion, ≈ *Ind. Ocean* ...30 H9
Reykjavik, *Iceland* ...6 D3
Rhein, ≈ *Europe* ...16 C3
Rheinland Pfalz, □ *Ger.* ...16 D3
Rhine = Rhein, ≈ *Ger.* ...16 C3
Rhode Island, □ *U.S.A.* ...37 B12
Rhodes = Ródhos, *Greece* ...15 F13
Rhodopi Planina, *Bulg.* ...15 D11
Rhön, *Ger.* ...16 C5
Rhondda, *U.K.* ...9 F4
Rhône, ≈ *France* ...12 D6
Rhum, *U.K.* ...10 E2
Ribeirão Prêto, *Brazil* ...41 H9
Richmond, *U.K.* ...9 F7
Richmond, *U.S.A.* ...37 C11
Riga, *Latvia* ...18 D3
Rijeka, *Croatia* ...14 B6
Rimini, *Italy* ...14 B5
Rio Branco, *Brazil* ...40 E5
Rio de Janeiro, *Brazil* ...41 H10
Rio Gallegos, *Argentina* ...42 G3
Rio Grande, *Brazil* ...42 C6
Rio Grande do Norte, □ *Brazil* ...41 E11
Rio Grande do Sul, □ *Brazil* ...42 B6
Rishiri-Tō, *Japan* ...21 E11
Riyadh = Ar Riyâd, *S. Arabia* ...25 C3
Rochefort, *France* ...12 D3
Rochester, *U.K.* ...9 F8
Rochester, *U.S.A.* ...37 B11
Rocky Mts., *N. Amer.* ...34 A4
Ródhos, *Greece* ...15 F13
Rogaland, □ *Norw.* ...7 G9
Roma, *Italy* ...14 C5
Romania, ■ *Europe* ...17 F12
Rondônia, □ *Brazil* ...40 F6
Roodepoort-Maraisburg, *S. Africa* ...29 K5
Roraima, □ *Brazil* ...40 C6
Rosario, *Argentina* ...42 C4
Roscommon, □ *Ire.* ...11 C3
Roseau, *Dominica* ...38 M20
Roskilde, *Den.* ...7 J12
Rostock, *Ger.* ...16 A6
Rostov, *Russia* ...18 E4
Rotherham, *U.K.* ...8 D6
Rotterdam, *Neth.* ...16 C2
Roubaix, *Belgium* ...16 C1
Rouen, *France* ...12 B4
Rousay, *U.K.* ...10 B5
Ruse, *Bulg.* ...15 C12
Russia, ■ *Europe/Asia* ...18 C10
Rwanda, ■ *Africa* ...28 E5

Ryde, *U.K.* ...9 G6

S

's-Gravenhage, *Neth.* ...16 B2
's-Hertogenbosch, *Neth.* ...16 C2
Saarbrucken, *Ger.* ...16 D3
Saarland, □ *Ger.* ...16 D3
Sabadell, *Spain* ...13 B6
Sabah, □ *Malaysia* ...23 C3
Sacramento, *U.S.A.* ...36 C3
Sado, *Japan* ...21 G10
Safi, *Morocco* ...26 B3
Saginaw, *U.S.A.* ...37 B10
Sahara, *Africa* ...26 D4
Saigon = Phanh Bho Ho Chi Minh, *Vietnam* ...23 B2
Saint John, *Canada* ...35 D13
Saintonge, □ *France* ...12 D3
Sakai, *Japan* ...21 B4
Sakata, *Japan* ...21 G10
Sakhalin, *Russia* ...19 D15
Salamanca, *Spain* ...13 B3
Salerno, *Italy* ...14 D6
Salford, *U.K.* ...8 D5
Salisbury, *U.K.* ...9 F6
Salt Lake City, *U.S.A.* ...36 B4
Salta, *Argentina* ...42 A3
Saltillo, *Mexico* ...38 B4
Salvador, *Brazil* ...41 F11
Salzburg, *Austria* ...16 E6
Salzgitter, *Ger.* ...16 B5
Samara, *Russia* ...18 D6
Samarkand, *Uzbekistan* ...18 F7
Samoan Is., *Pac. Ocean* ...31 A12
Sámos, *Greece* ...15 F12
Samothráki, *Greece* ...15 D11
San Angelo, *U.S.A.* ...36 D6
San Antonio, *U.S.A.* ...36 E7
San Cristóbal, *Venezuela* ...40 B4
San Diego, *U.S.A.* ...36 D3
San Fernando, *Trinidad* ...38 S20
San Francisco, *U.S.A.* ...36 C2
San Francisco de Macoris, *Dom. Rep.* ...39 D10
San Jose, *U.S.A.* ...36 C2
San Juan, *Argentina* ...42 C3
San Juan, *Puerto Rico* ...39 D11
San Luis Potosi, *Mexico* ...38 C4
San Marino, ■ *Europe* ...14 C5
San Miguel de Tucuman, *Argentina* 42 B3
San Salvador, *El Salvador* ...38 E7
San Sebastian, *Spain* ...13 A4
San'a, *Yemen* ...25 D3
Sancti Spiritus, *Cuba* ...39 C9
Sanday, *U.K.* ...10 B6
Santa Ana, *U.S.A.* ...36 D3
Santa Barbara, *U.S.A.* ...36 D3
Santa Catarina, □ *Brazil* ...42 B7
Santa Clara, *Cuba* ...39 C9
Santa Clara, *U.S.A.* ...36 C2
Santa Cruz, *Bolivia* ...40 G6
Santa Cruz, *Canary Is.* ...26 C1
Santa Fe, *Argentina* ...42 C4
Santa Marta, *Colombia* ...40 A4
Santander, *Spain* ...13 A4
Santarém, *Brazil* ...41 D8
Santarem, *Port.* ...13 C1
Santiago, *Chile* ...42 C2
Santiago, *Dom. Rep.* ...39 D10
Santiago, *Spain* ...13 A1
Santiago de Cuba, *Cuba* ...39 C9
Santo Domingo, *Dom. Rep.* ...39 D11
Santos, *Brazil* ...42 A7
São Francisco, ≈ *Brazil* ...41 F11
São Luís, *Brazil* ...41 D10
São Paulo, □ *Brazil* ...41 H9
São Paulo, *Brazil* ...42 A7
São Tomé & Principe, ■ *Africa* ...30 E4
Sapporo, *Japan* ...21 F11
Sarajevo, *Bosnia* ...15 C8
Saratov, *Russia* ...18 D5
Sarawak, □ *Malaysia* ...23 C3
Sardegna, □ *Italy* ...14 D3
Sardinia = Sardegna, □ *Italy* ...14 D3
Sark, *Channel Is.* ...12 B2
Sasebo, *Japan* ...21 C1
Saskatchewan, □ *Canada* ...34 C9
Saskatoon, *Canada* ...34 C9
Satu Mare, *Rom.* ...17 E11
Saudi Arabia, ■ *Asia* ...25 C3
Sault Ste. Marie, *Canada* ...35 D11
Savannah, *U.S.A.* ...37 D10
Savoie, □ *France* ...12 D7
Savona, *Italy* ...14 B3
Scapa Flow, *U.K.* ...10 C5
Scarborough, *U.K.* ...8 C7
Schleswig - Holstein, □ *Ger.* ...16 A4
Schwäbische Alb, *Ger.* ...16 D4
Schwarzwald, *Ger.* ...16 D4
Schwerin, *Ger.* ...16 B5
Scilly, Is. of, *U.K.* ...9 H2
Scotland, □ *U.K.* ...10 E4
Scunthorpe, *U.K.* ...8 D7
Seattle, *U.S.A.* ...36 A2
Segovia, *Spain* ...13 B3
Seine, ≈ *France* ...12 B4
Sekondi - Takoradi, *Ghana* ...26 H4
Selkirk, *U.K.* ...10 F6

Semarang, *Indonesia* ...23 D3
Sendai, *Japan* ...21 G11
Senegal, ■ *Africa* ...26 F2
Serbia, □ *Yug.* ...15 C9
Setonaikai, *Japan* ...21 C3
Setúbal, *Port.* ...13 C1
Sevastopol, *Ukraine* ...18 E4
Severn, ≈ *U.K.* ...9 F5
Severnaya Zemlya, *Russia* ...19 B10
Sevilla, *Spain* ...13 D3
Seychelles, ■ *Ind. Ocean* ...3 E12
Sfax, *Tunisia* ...27 B7
Shache, *China* ...22 C2
Shanghai, *China* ...22 C7
Shannon, ≈ *Ire.* ...11 D2
Shantou, *China* ...22 D6
Shapinsay, *U.K.* ...10 B6
Sheffield, *U.K.* ...8 D6
Shenyang, *China* ...22 B7
Sherwood Forest, *U.K.* ...8 D6
Shetland, □ *U.K.* ...10 A7
Shikoku, *Japan* ...21 C3
Shimonoseki, *Japan* ...21 C2
Shirāz, *Iran* ...25 C4
Shizuoka, *Japan* ...21 B6
Sholapur, *India* ...24 E4
Shreveport, *U.S.A.* ...37 D8
Shrewsbury, *U.K.* ...8 E5
Shropshire, □ *U.K.* ...9 E5
Siam = Thailand, ■ *Asia* ...23 B2
Sibiu, *Rom.* ...17 F12
Sichuan, □ *China* ...22 D5
Sicilia, □ *Italy* ...14 F5
Siena, *Italy* ...14 C4
Sierra Leone, ■ *Africa* ...26 G2
Sierra Nevada, *U.S.A.* ...36 C3
Silver City, *Panama* ...38 H14
Simpson Desert, *Australia* ...32 C6
Singapore, ■ *Asia* ...23 C2
Sioux City, *U.S.A.* ...37 B7
Sioux Falls, *U.S.A.* ...37 B7
Siracusa, *Italy* ...14 F6
Sitges, *Spain* ...13 B6
Sjælland, *Den.* ...7 J11
Skagerrak, *Europe* ...7 H10
Skien, *Norw.* ...7 G10
Skikda, *Algeria* ...26 A6
Skopje, *Macedonia* ...15 C9
Skye, I. of, *U.K.* ...10 D2
Slieve Aughty, *Ire.* ...11 C3
Slieve Bloom, *Ire.* ...11 C4
Slieve Mish, *Ire.* ...11 D2
Sligo, *Ire.* ...11 B3
Slough, *U.K.* ...9 F7
Slovak Rep., ■ *Europe* ...17 D9
Slovenia, ■ *Europe* ...14 B6
Snake, ≈ *U.S.A.* ...36 A3
Snowdon, *U.K.* ...8 D3
Society Is., *Pac. Ocean* ...2 E2
Socotra, *Yemen* ...25 D4
Söderhamn, *Swed.* ...7 F14
Sofiya, *Bulg.* ...15 C10
Sogn og Fjordane, □ *Norw.* ...7 F9
Solimoes, ≈ *Brazil* ...40 D5
Solomon Is., ■ *Pac. Ocean* ...3 E17
Solway Firth, *U.K.* ...8 C4
Somali Rep., ■ *Africa* ...30 E8
Somerset, □ *U.K.* ...9 F4
Somerset I., *Canada* ...34 A10
Sør-Trondelag, □ *Norw.* ...6 D12
Soria, *Spain* ...13 B4
Sorocaba, *Brazil* ...42 A7
Sosnowiec, *Poland* ...17 C9
Sôul, *S. Korea* ...22 C7
Sousse, *Tunisia* ...27 A7
South Africa, ■ *Africa* ...29 L3
South Australia, □ *Australia* ...32 D5
South Bend, *U.S.A.* ...37 B9
South Carolina, □ *U.S.A.* ...37 D10
South China Sea, *Asia* ...23 B3
South Dakota, □ *U.S.A.* ...36 B6
South Downs, *U.K.* ...9 G7
South Georgia, *Atl. Ocean* ...42 G9
South Glamorgan, □ *U.K.* ...9 F4
South Island, *N.Z.* ...31 K3
South Korea, ■ *Asia* ...22 C7
South Ronaldsay, *U.K.* ...10 C6
South Shields, *U.K.* ...8 C6
South Uist, *U.K.* ...10 D1
South Yorkshire, □ *U.K.* ...8 D6
Southampton, *U.K.* ...9 G6
Southampton I., *Canada* ...35 B11
Southend, *U.K.* ...9 F8
Southern Alps, *N.Z.* ...31 K3
Southern Ocean, ...3 G12
Southern Uplands, *U.K.* ...10 F5
Southport, *U.K.* ...8 D4
Soutpansberge, *S. Africa* ...29 J5
Spain, ■ *Europe* ...13 B4
Spandau, *Ger.* ...16 B6
Spanish Town, *Jamaica* ...38 K17
Spencer Gulf, *Australia* ...32 E6
Sperrin Mts., *U.K.* ...11 B4
Spessart, *Ger.* ...16 C5
Split, *Croatia* ...14 C7
Spokane, *U.S.A.* ...36 A3
Sporádhes Voríai, *Greece* ...15 E11
Springfield, *U.S.A.* ...37 B12
Springs, *S. Africa* ...29 K5

Index

Sri Lanka, ■ *Asia* ...24 G5
Srinagar, *India* ...24 B3
St. Albans, *U.K.* ...9 F7
St. Andrews, *U.K.* ...10 E6
St. Austell, *U.K.* ...9 G3
St. Boniface, *Canada* ...34 D10
St. Christopher-Nevis = St. Kitts -
　Nevis, ■ *W. Indies* ...38 K19
St. Croix, *W. Indies* ...39 D12
St. - Étienne, *France* ...12 D6
St. Gallen, *Switz.* ...16 E4
St. George's, *Grenada* ...38 Q20
St. George's Channel, *Europe* ...11 E5
St. Helena, *Atl. Ocean* ...30 G3
St. Helens, *U.K.* ...8 D5
St. John's, *Antigua* ...38 K20
St. John's, *Canada* ...35 D14
St. Kitts - Nevis, ■ *W. Indies* ...38 K19
St. Lawrence, ≈ *Canada* ...35 D14
St. Louis, *U.S.A.* ...37 C8
St. Lucia, ■ *W. Indies* ...38 P21
St. Maarten, □ *W. Indies* ...38 J18
St. Malo, *France* ...12 B2
St. Martin, □ *W. Indies* ...38 J18
St. Michael's Mt., *U.K.* ...9 G2
St. Nazaire, *France* ...12 C2
St. Paul, *U.S.A.* ...37 B8
St. Peterburg, *Russia* ...18 D4
St. Petersburg, *U.S.A.* ...37 E10
St. Pierre et Miquelon, □ *N. Amer.* .35 D14
St. Thomas, *W. Indies* ...39 D12
St. - Denis, *France* ...12 B5
St. - Tropez, *France* ...12 E7
St. Vincent & the Grenadines,
　■ *W. Indies* ...38 P20
Stafford, *U.K.* ...8 E5
Staffordshire, □ *U.K.* ...8 E5
Staines, *U.K.* ...9 F7
Stalingrad = Volgograd, *Russia* ...18 E5
Stanley, *Falkland Is.* ...42 G5
Stara Planina, *Bulg.* ...15 C11
Stavanger, *Norw.* ...7 G8
Steiermark, □ *Austria* ...16 E7
Sterea Ellas, □ *Greece* ...15 E9
Stewart I., *N.Z.* ...31 M1
Stirling, *U.K.* ...10 E5
Stockholm, *Swed.* ...7 G15
Stockport, *U.K.* ...8 D5
Stockton, *U.K.* ...8 C6
Stockton, *U.S.A.* ...36 C2
Stoke-on-Trent, *U.K.* ...8 D5
Stonehenge, *U.K.* ...9 F6
Stourbridge, *U.K.* ...9 E5
Strabane, *U.K.* ...11 B4
Stralsund, *Ger.* ...16 A6
Strasbourg, *France* ...12 B7
Stratford-on-Avon, *U.K.* ...9 E6
Strath Spey, *U.K.* ...10 D5
Strathclyde, □ *U.K.* ...10 F3
Stromeferry, *U.K.* ...10 D3
Stronsay, *U.K.* ...10 B6
Stuttgart, *Ger.* ...16 D4
Subotica, *Yug.* ...15 A8
Sucre, *Bolivia* ...40 G5
Sudan, ■ *Africa* ...27 E10
Sudbury, *Canada* ...35 D11
Suez Canal, *Egypt* ...25 B2
Suez = El Suweis, *Egypt* ...27 C11
Suffolk, □ *U.K.* ...9 E8
Sulawesi, *Indonesia* ...23 D4
Sumatera, *Indonesia* ...23 D2
Sumba, *Indonesia* ...23 D4
Sumbawa, *Indonesia* ...23 D3
Sunderland, *U.K.* ...8 C6
Sundsvall, *Swed.* ...6 E14
Superior, L., *N. Amer.* ...37 A9
Surabaja, *Indonesia* ...23 D3
Surat, *India* ...24 D3
Surinam, ■ *S. Amer.* ...41 C7
Surrey, □ *U.K.* ...9 F7
Sutton-in-Ashfield, *U.K.* ...8 D6
Suva, *Fiji* ...31 D8
Suzhou, *China* ...22 C7
Svendborg, *Den.* ...7 J11
Sverdlovsk = Yekaterinburg, *Russia* 18 D7
Swansea, *U.K.* ...9 F4
Swaziland, ■ *Africa* ...29 K6
Sweden, ■ *Europe* ...7 F13
Swindon, *U.K.* ...9 F6
Switzerland, ■ *Europe* ...16 E3
Sydney, *Australia* ...33 E9
Syracuse, *U.S.A.* ...37 B11
Syria, ■ *Asia* ...25 B2
Syrian Desert, *Asia* ...25 B2
Szczecin, *Poland* ...16 B7
Szeged, *Hungary* ...17 E10

T
Tabrīz, *Iran* ...25 B3
Tacoma, *U.S.A.* ...36 A2
Taegu, *S. Korea* ...22 C7
Tahiti, *Pac. Ocean* ...2 E2
Taibei, *Taiwan* ...22 D7
Tainan, *Taiwan* ...22 D7
Taiwan, ■ *Asia* ...22 D7
Taiyuan, *China* ...22 C6
Taizhong, *Taiwan* ...22 D7
Tajikistan, ■ *Asia* ...18 F7

Takamatsu, *Japan* ...21 B4
Talcahuano, *Chile* ...42 D2
Tallinn, *Estonia* ...18 D3
Tamil Nadu, □ *India* ...24 F4
Tampa, *U.S.A.* ...37 E10
Tampere, *Fin.* ...7 F17
Tampico, *Mexico* ...38 C5
Tamworth, *U.K.* ...9 E6
Tane-ga-Shima, *Japan* ...21 D2
Tanga, *Tanzania* ...28 F7
Tanganyika, L., *Africa* ...28 F5
Tanger, *Morocco* ...26 A3
Tangshan, *China* ...22 C6
Tanimbar Is., *Indonesia* ...23 D5
Tanta, *Egypt* ...27 B11
Tanzania, ■ *Africa* ...28 F7
Tarābulus, *Lebanon* ...25 B2
Tarābulus, *Libya* ...27 B7
Taranto, *Italy* ...14 D7
Tarragona, *Spain* ...13 B6
Tarrasa, *Spain* ...13 B6
Tashkent, *Uzbekistan* ...18 E7
Tasman Sea, *Pac. Ocean* ...31 J2
Tasmania, *Australia* ...33 G8
Tauern, *Austria* ...16 E6
Taunton, *U.K.* ...9 F4
Taunus, *Ger.* ...16 C4
Tay, ≈ *U.K.* ...10 E5
Tayside, □ *U.K.* ...10 E5
Tbilisi, *Georgia* ...18 E5
Tchad, L., *Chad* ...27 F7
Teeside, *U.K.* ...8 C6
Tegucigalpa, *Honduras* ...38 E7
Tehrān, *Iran* ...25 B4
Tehuantepec, Istme de, *Mexico* ...38 D5
Tejo, ≈ *Port.* ...13 C1
Tel Aviv - Yafo, *Israel* ...25 B2
Telemark, □ *Norw.* ...7 G10
Telford, *U.K.* ...8 E5
Tenerife, *Canary Is.* ...26 C1
Tennessee, □ *U.S.A.* ...37 C9
Tennessee, ≈ *U.S.A.* ...37 C9
Teresina, *Brazil* ...41 E10
Terni, *Italy* ...14 C5
Teruel, *Spain* ...13 B5
Tetouan, *Morocco* ...26 A3
Teutoburger Wald, *Ger.* ...16 B4
Tevere, ≈ *Italy* ...14 C5
Texas, □ *U.S.A.* ...36 D6
Thailand, ■ *Asia* ...23 B2
Thames, ≈ *U.K.* ...9 F8
Thásos, *Greece* ...15 D11
The Hague = 's-Gravenhage, *Neth.* .16 B2
Thessalia, □ *Greece* ...15 E10
Thessaloníka, *Greece* ...15 D10
Thies, *Senegal* ...26 F1
Thráki, □ *Greece* ...15 D11
Thunder Bay, *Canada* ...35 D11
Thüringer Wald, *Ger.* ...16 C5
Thurles, *Ire.* ...11 D4
Thurso, *U.K.* ...10 C5
Tianjin, *China* ...22 C6
Tiber = Tevere, ≈ *Italy* ...14 C5
Tibesti, *Chad* ...27 D8
Tibet = Xizang, □ *China* ...22 C3
Tientsin = Tianjin, *China* ...22 C6
Tierra del Fuego, *S. Amer.* ...42 G3
Tigris, ≈ *Iraq* ...25 B3
Tijuana, *Mexico* ...38 A1
Tilburg, *Neth.* ...16 C2
Timaru, *N.Z.* ...31 L3
Timişoara, *Rom.* ...17 F10
Timor, *Indonesia* ...23 D4
Tínos, *Greece* ...15 F11
Tipperary, □ *Ire.* ...11 D4
Tipperary, *Ire.* ...11 D3
Tipton, *U.K.* ...9 E5
Tirana, *Alb.* ...15 D8
Tirol, □ *Austria* ...16 E5
Tiruchchirappalli, *India* ...24 F4
Tiree, *U.K.* ...10 E2
Titicaca, L., *S. Amer.* ...40 G5
Titograd = Podgorica, *Yug.* ...15 C8
Tizi-Ouzou, *Algeria* ...26 A5
Tobago, *W. Indies* ...39 E12
Togo, ■ *Africa* ...26 G5
Tokelau Is., *Pac. Ocean* ...2 E1
Tōkyō, *Japan* ...21 B6
Toledo, *Spain* ...13 C3
Toledo, *U.S.A.* ...37 B10
Toluca, *Mexico* ...38 D5
Tomsk, *Russia* ...18 D9
Tonga, ■ *Pac. Ocean* ...31 D11
Toowoomba, *Australia* ...33 D9
Topeka, *U.S.A.* ...37 C7
Torbay, *U.K.* ...9 G4
Torino, *Italy* ...14 B2
Toronto, *Canada* ...35 D12
Torquay, *U.K.* ...9 G4
Torrens, L., *Australia* ...33 E6
Torremolinos, *Spain* ...13 D3
Torreón, *Mexico* ...38 B4
Tortosa, *Spain* ...13 B6
Toscana, □ *Italy* ...14 C4
Toulon, *France* ...12 E6
Toulouse, *France* ...12 E4
Touraine, □ *France* ...12 C4
Tourcoing, *Belgium* ...16 C1

Tours, *France* ...12 C4
Townsville, *Australia* ...33 B8
Toyama, *Japan* ...21 A5
Toyohashi, *Japan* ...21 B5
Toyonaka, *Japan* ...21 B4
Tralee, *Ire.* ...11 D2
Transilvania, *Rom.* ...17 E12
Transvaal, □ *S. Africa* ...29 K5
Trápani, *Italy* ...14 E5
Trelleborg, *Swed.* ...7 J12
Trentino Alto-Adige, □ *Italy* ...14 A4
Treviso, *Italy* ...14 B5
Trier, *Ger.* ...16 D3
Trieste, *Italy* ...14 B5
Trincomalee, *Sri Lanka* ...24 G5
Trinidad & Tobago, ■ *W. Indies* ...39 E12
Tripoli = Tarābulus, *Libya* ...27 B7
Tristan da Cunha, *Atl. Ocean* ...2 F9
Trois-Rivières, *Canada* ...35 D12
Trollhättan, *Swed.* ...7 G12
Troms, □ *Norw.* ...6 B15
Tromso, *Norw.* ...6 B15
Trondheim, *Norw.* ...6 E11
Trossachs, *U.K.* ...10 E4
Trujillo, *Peru* ...40 E3
Tsugaru-Kaikyō, *Japan* ...21 F11
Tsushima, *Japan* ...21 H8
Tuamotu Arch, *Pac. Ocean* ...2 E3
Tubuai Is., *Pac. Ocean* ...2 F7
Tucson, *U.S.A.* ...36 D4
Tula, *Russia* ...18 D4
Tullamore, *Ire.* ...11 C4
Tulsa, *U.S.A.* ...37 C7
Tulua, *Colombia* ...40 C3
Tunis, *Tunisia* ...26 A6
Tunisia, ■ *Africa* ...26 A6
Turin = Torino, *Italy* ...14 B2
Turkana, L., *Kenya* ...28 D7
Turkey, ■ *Asia* ...25 B2
Turkmenistan, ■ *Asia* ...18 F6
Turku, *Fin.* ...7 F17
Turnu-Severin, *Rom.* ...17 F11
Turun ja Pori, *Fin.* ...7 F17
Tuvalu, ■ *Pac. Ocean* ...3 E18
Tver, *Russia* ...18 D4
Tyler, *U.S.A.* ...37 D7
Tyne & Wear, □ *U.K.* ...8 C6
Tynemouth, *U.K.* ...8 C6
Tyrrhenian Sea, *Italy* ...14 E5

U
Uberaba, *Brazil* ...41 G9
Uddevalla, *Swed.* ...7 G11
Udine, *Italy* ...14 A5
Ufa, *Russia* ...18 D6
Uganda, ■ *Africa* ...28 D6
Ujpest, *Hungary* ...17 E9
Ujung Pandang, *Indonesia* ...23 D3
Ukraine, ■ *Europe* ...18 E4
Ulaanbaatar, *Mong.* ...22 B5
Ulan Ude, *Russia* ...19 D11
Ullapool, *U.K.* ...10 D3
Ulm, *Ger.* ...16 D4
Ulster, *U.K.* ...11 B4
Umbria, □ *Italy* ...14 C5
Ungava Pen., *Canada* ...35 C12
United Arab Emirates, ■ *Asia* ...25 C4
United Kingdom, ■ *Europe* ...4 E5
United States of America, ■
　N. Amer. ...36 C6
Unst, *U.K.* ...10 A8
Uppsala, *Swed.* ...7 G14
Urmia, L., *Iran* ...25 B3
Uruguay, ■ *S. Amer.* ...42 C5
Uruguay, ≈ *S. Amer.* ...42 C5
Urumqi, *China* ...22 B3
Usti nad Labem, *Czech Rep.* ...16 C7
Utah, □ *U.S.A.* ...36 C4
Utrecht, *Neth.* ...16 B2
Utsunomiya, *Japan* ...21 A6
Uttar Pradesh, □ *India* ...24 C5
Uudenmaa, □ *Fin.* ...7 F18
Uzbekistan, ■ *Asia* ...18 E7

V
Vaal, ≈ *S. Africa* ...29 K4
Vaasa, □ *Fin.* ...6 E17
Vadso, *Norw.* ...6 A20
Valence, *France* ...12 D6
Valencia, □ *Spain* ...13 C5
Valencia, *Spain* ...13 C5
Valencia, *Venezuela* ...40 A5
Valladolid, *Spain* ...13 B3
Valle d'Aosta, □ *Italy* ...14 B2
Valletta, *Malta* ...14 G6
Valparaíso, *Chile* ...42 C2
Vancouver, *Canada* ...34 D7
Vancouver I., *Canada* ...34 D7
Vanuatu, ■ *Pac. Ocean* ...3 E18
Varanasi, *India* ...24 C5
Värmland, □ *Swed.* ...7 G12
Varna, *Bulg.* ...15 C12
Västerås, *Swed.* ...7 G14
Vasterbotten, □ *Norw.* ...6 D14
Vasternorrland, □ *Norw.* ...6 E14
Västervik, *Swed.* ...7 H14
Västmanland, □ *Swed.* ...7 G14

Vatnajökull, *Iceland* ...6 D5
Veneto, □ *Italy* ...14 B4
Venézia, *Italy* ...14 B5
Venezuela, ■ *S. Amer.* ...40 B5
Veracruz, *Mexico* ...38 D5
Vereeniging, *S. Africa* ...29 K5
Vermont, □ *U.S.A.* ...37 B12
Verona, *Italy* ...14 B4
Versailles, *France* ...12 B5
Vest-Agder, □ *Norw.* ...7 G9
Vesterålen, *Norw.* ...6 B13
Vestfjorden, *Norw.* ...6 B13
Vesuvio, *Italy* ...14 D6
Viborg, *Den.* ...7 H10
Vichy, *France* ...12 C5
Victoria, *Australia* ...33 F7
Victoria, *Canada* ...34 D7
Victoria Falls, *Zimbabwe* ...29 H5
Victoria I., *Canada* ...34 A8
Victoria, L., *Africa* ...28 E6
Vienna = Wien, *Austria* ...16 D8
Vientos, Paso de los, *W. Indies* ...39 C10
Vietnam, ■ *Asia* ...23 B2
Vigo, *Spain* ...13 A1
Viña del Mar, *Chile* ...42 C2
Virgin Is., *W. Indies* ...39 D12
Virginia, □ *U.S.A.* ...37 C11
Visby, *Swed.* ...7 H15
Vitória, *Brazil* ...41 H10
Vitoria, *Spain* ...13 A4
Vladivostok, *Russia* ...19 E14
Vojvodina, □ *Yug.* ...15 B8
Volga, ≈ *Russia* ...18 E5
Volgograd, *Russia* ...18 E5
Vólos, *Greece* ...15 E10
Volta, L., *Ghana* ...26 G4
Vorarlberg, □ *Austria* ...16 E4
Voronezh, *Russia* ...18 D4
Vyatka, *Russia* ...18 D5

W
Waco, *U.S.A.* ...37 D7
Wâd Medanî, *Sudan* ...27 F11
Wakayama, *Japan* ...21 B4
Wakefield, *U.K.* ...8 D6
Wakkanai, *Japan* ...21 E11
Wales, □ *U.K.* ...9 E4
Wallasey, *U.K.* ...8 D4
Wallsend, *U.K.* ...8 B6
Walney, I., *U.K.* ...8 C4
Walsall, *U.K.* ...9 E6
Walvisbaai, *S. Africa* ...29 J2
Wanganui, *N.Z.* ...31 H5
Warley, *U.K.* ...9 E6
Warrington, *U.K.* ...8 D5
Warszawa, *Poland* ...17 B10
Warwick, *U.K.* ...9 E6
Warwickshire, □ *U.K.* ...9 E6
Wash, The, *U.K.* ...8 E8
Washington, □ *U.S.A.* ...36 A2
Washington D.C., *U.S.A.* ...37 C11
Waterbury, *U.S.A.* ...37 B12
Waterford, *Ire.* ...11 D4
Watford, *U.K.* ...9 F7
Weald, The, *U.K.* ...9 F7
Welkom, *S. Africa* ...29 K5
Wellesley Is., *Australia* ...33 B6
Wellington, *N.Z.* ...31 J5
Wellington I., *Chile* ...42 F2
Wenzhou, *China* ...22 D7
West Bromwich, *U.K.* ...9 E5
West Glamorgan, □ *U.K.* ...9 F4
West Indies ...39 D10
West Midlands, □ *U.K.* ...9 E6
West Sussex, □ *U.K.* ...9 G7
West Virginia, □ *U.S.A.* ...37 C10
West Yorkshire, □ *U.K.* ...8 D6
Western Australia, □ *Oceania* ...32 C3
Western Is., □ *U.K.* ...10 D1
Western Sahara, ■ *Africa* ...26 C2
Western Samoa, ■ *Pac. Ocean* ...2 E1
Westerwald, *Ger.* ...16 C3
Westmeath, □ *Ire.* ...11 C4
Weston-super-Mare, *U.K.* ...9 F6
Westray, *U.K.* ...10 B5
Wexford, *Ire.* ...11 D5
Weymouth, *U.K.* ...9 G5
Whalsay, *U.K.* ...10 A8
White Nile = Nîl el Abyad, ≈ *Africa* ...27 E11
White Sea = Beloye More, *Russia* ...18 C4
Whitehaven, *U.K.* ...8 C4
Whitehorse, *Canada* ...34 B6
Wichita, *U.S.A.* ...37 C7
Wichita Falls, *U.S.A.* ...36 D7
Wick, *U.K.* ...10 C5
Wicklow, *Ire.* ...11 D5
Wien, *Austria* ...16 D8
Wiesbaden, *Ger.* ...16 C4
Wigan, *U.K.* ...8 D5
Wight, I. of, □ *U.K.* ...9 G6
Wilhelmshaven, *Ger.* ...16 B4
Wilmington, *U.S.A.* ...37 C11
Wiltshire, □ *U.K.* ...9 F6
Winchester, *U.K.* ...9 F6
Windermere, L., *U.K.* ...8 C5

Windsor, *U.K.* ...9 F7
Windsor, *Canada* ...35 D11
Windward Is., *W. Indies* ...39 E12
Winnipeg, *Canada* ...34 D10
Winnipeg, L., *Canada* ...34 C10
Winston Salem, *U.S.A.* ...37 C10
Winterthur, *Switz.* ...16 E4
Wirral, The, *U.K.* ...8 D4
Wisconsin, □ *U.S.A.* ...37 B9
Wishaw, *U.K.* ...10 F5
Włocławek, *Poland* ...17 B9
Woking, *U.K.* ...9 F7
Wollongong, *Australia* ...33 E9
Wolverhampton, *U.K.* ...9 E5
Worcester, *U.K.* ...9 E5
Worcester, *U.S.A.* ...37 B12
Workington, *U.K.* ...8 C4
Worksop, *U.K.* ...8 D6
Worms, *Ger.* ...16 D4
Worthing, *U.K.* ...9 G7
Wrexham, *U.K.* ...8 D4
Wrocław, *Poland* ...16 C8
Wuhan, *China* ...22 C6
Wuhu, *China* ...22 C6
Wuppertal, *Ger.* ...16 C3
Würzburg, *Ger.* ...16 D4
Wyoming, □ *U.S.A.* ...36 B5

X
Xi'an, *China* ...22 C5
Xiaguan, *China* ...22 D5
Xingu, ≈ *Brazil* ...41 D8
Xinjiang Uygur, □ *China* ...22 B3
Xizang, □ *China* ...22 C3
Xuzhou, *China* ...22 C6

Y
Yakushima, *Japan* ...21 D2
Yakutsk, *Russia* ...19 C13
Yamagata, *Japan* ...21 G11
Yaoundé, *Cameroon* ...28 D2
Yaroslavl, *Russia* ...18 D4
Yazd, *Iran* ...25 B4
Yell, *U.K.* ...10 A7
Yellow Sea, *Asia* ...22 C7
Yellowknife, *Canada* ...34 B8
Yellowstone National Park, *U.S.A.* ...36 B4
Yemen, ■ *Asia* ...25 D3
Yenisey, ≈ *Russia* ...18 C9
Yeovil, *U.K.* ...9 G5
Yerevan, *Armenia* ...18 E5
Yining, *China* ...22 B3
Yokohama, *Japan* ...21 B6
Yokosuka, *Japan* ...21 B6
York, *U.K.* ...8 D6
Youghal, *Ire.* ...11 E4
Ystad, *Swed.* ...7 J12
Yucatan, □ *Mexico* ...38 D7
Yugoslavia, ■ *Europe* ...15 B9
Yukon, ≈ *N. Amer.* ...34 B4
Yukon Territory, □ *Canada* ...34 B6

Z
Zabrze, *Poland* ...17 C9
Zagazig, *Egypt* ...27 B11
Zagreb, *Croatia* ...14 B6
Zagros Mts., *Iran* ...25 B3
Zaïre, ≈ *Africa* ...28 D4
Zaïre, ■ *Africa* ...28 E4
Zákinthos, *Greece* ...15 F9
Zambezi, ≈ *Africa* ...29 H6
Zambia, ■ *Africa* ...29 G5
Zamora, *Spain* ...13 B3
Zanzibar, *Tanzania* ...28 F7
Zaporozhye, *Ukraine* ...18 E4
Zaragoza, *Spain* ...13 B5
Zaria, *Nigeria* ...26 F6
Zemlya Frantsa Iosifa, *Russia* ...18 B6
Zhanghua, *Taiwan* ...22 D7
Zhangjiakou, *China* ...22 B6
Zhengzhou, *China* ...22 C6
Zhenjiang, *China* ...22 C6
Zibo, *China* ...22 C6
Zigong, *China* ...22 D5
Zimbabwe, ■ *Africa* ...29 H5
Zürich, *Switz.* ...16 E4
Zwickau, *Ger.* ...16 C6